Praise for *When Others Shuddered*

Warning: This book might just change your life. These women will inspire you to ask God that your life might count for His kingdom—whatever the cost. No woman is too young or too old, too poor or too rich to become a mighty vessel in the hands of the Lord. "Here am I Lord send me!"

—**DR. JULI SLATTERY**, Clinical psychologist, Author,
   President and Co-founder of Authentic Intimacy, MBI Trustee

I was one of four sons and the father of three, never wanting for great role models. As the grandfather of three granddaughters, however, I'm constantly scouring the media landscape for true stories of women my young beloveds can aspire to emulate. *When Others Shuddered* fills the bill. I love everything about this book, from the women Jamie Janosz chose to the quirky design, and from the stories themselves to the resolve they inspire in me. Imagine the impact such a work can have on the lives of young women.

—**JERRY B. JENKINS**, Novelist & Biographer,
   Owner, Christian Writers Guild

WHEN OTHERS SHUDDERED

EIGHT WOMEN WHO REFUSED TO GIVE UP

JAMIE JANOSZ

MOODY PUBLISHERS
CHICAGO

Scripture quotations are taken from the King James Version.

Edited by: Karen L. Waddles
Interior design: Design Corps
Cover design: Erik M. Peterson
Cover title design: Jonathan Critcher
Cover photo of woman copyright © 2010 by duncan 1890/iStockphoto. All rights reserved.
Author photo: Jill Obermaier

All websites and phone numbers listed herein are accurate at the time of publication but may change in the future or cease to exist. The listing of website references and resources does not imply publisher endorsement of the site's entire contents. Groups and organizations are listed for informational purposes, and listing does not imply publisher endorsement of their activities.

ISBN 978-0-8024-1078-8

We hope you enjoy this book from Moody Publishers. Our goal is to provide high-quality, thought-provoking books and products that connect truth to your real needs and challenges. For more information on other books and products written and produced from a biblical perspective, go to www.moodypublishers.com or write to:

Moody Publishers
820 N. LaSalle Boulevard
Chicago, IL 60610

1 3 5 7 9 10 8 6 4 2

Printed in the United States of America

—⦿——⧼⧽⧼⧽——⦿—

To my mom,
whose courage, energy,
and faith inspire me,
and to my husband, Milt,
whose love gives me strength.

—⦿——⧼⧽⧼⧽——⦿—

Contents

FANNY CROSBY
1820–1915

"EMMA" EMELINE E. DRYER
1835–1925

"NETTIE" NANCY (FOWLER) MCCORMICK
1835–1923

SARAH DUNN CLARKE
1835–1918

AMANDA SMITH
1837–1915

VIRGINIA ASHER
1869–1937

EVANGELINE BOOTH
1865–1950

MARY MCLEOD BETHUNE
1875–1955

FOREWORD

As a woman, I count it a privilege to write the foreword to this book about Christian women who are part of our spiritual history. This is a story about God's work on earth through some of His disciples. Jesus always had a heart for women despite the adverse culture of His day. He broke all the norms of His society by inviting them to join His traveling team, listen to His teaching, and minister to the poorest of the poor, the sick and the outcasts, the abused and needy.

What joy to my heart to be reminded of people and stories I have known, and others I have now been introduced to. Looking through the window of my soon-to-be eighties, "I want to be like them when I grow up!"

Many of us are familiar with the better-known heroes of the faith. But reading along in this book and being introduced to new friends like Sarah Dunn Clarke, Amanda Smith, Nettie McCormick, and other legends, I have to admit I have been tempted to wish for another life! So many are the lost, so lost are the many: so lonely and yet so reachable by the arms of our love are the unlovable. Love, we are told, never fails. I learned this phrase does not mean "love never fails to get a positive response." Rather that God's love continues on whether the loved one ever responds or not!

These real women, whose stories have been so well told, spent their lives totally sold-out for Him, whether their practical love was spurned or responded to. They stir the embers of our faith, firing up our resolve to keep following Jesus as we meet them between these pages, and they call us to uncompromising commitment. In the end, what else is there?

Read this book with a hearing heart and a ready willingness to follow in their way! May God raise up an army of women in this generation: Jesus lovers and Glory givers who will match the fire of devotion that is recounted here.

—JILL BRISCOE

They Refused to Give Up

W e have too few female heroes of the faith.

It is easy to name men who have worked for God in historic and substantial ways, but very often, when asked to name a notable woman of faith, our minds draw a collective blank.

Why?

Certainly it is not for lack of women who have served God.

Rather, I think it is because these women's names are not well known. They often worked quietly behind the scenes. Their names did not make headlines. Their achievements were not recorded in history books. They did not seek the spotlight. Their acts of service reached into areas of society where others did not want to tread and, maybe, preferred not to talk about.

These were ordinary women who felt called by God to do extraordinary tasks. They walked into tawdry saloons and sang hymns. They faced off with gangsters in the Western frontier. They prayed with prostitutes in urban brothels. They traveled by coach and steamer to the urban centers of turn-of-the-century America. They were the first responders to great disasters like the Chicago fire and the San Francisco earthquake. They fought the violent prejudice of the Ku Klux Klan and the mistreatment of women and children in industrial factories.

They were compassionate and called, defending what they knew was right.

They were gutsy women who acted an awful lot like Jesus—giving their lives to serve a sinful and broken world.

These women did quiet things. They wrote checks and made sure their gifts were used effectively. They attended church and mission services night after night, no matter how exhausted they became. They knocked on the doors of homes, sitting with women of all races and ages and economic levels. They entered the most wretched slums of our cities, visiting factories and villages, working in rescue missions until the wee hours of the morning. They pinched pennies and walked for miles, giving their money to support God's work.

These women were also completely human. They experienced the devastating deaths of their children and the heartrending failures of marriage. They had their dreams snatched away, and their abilities discounted. They sometimes spoke too sharply or demanded too little. Their health sometimes forced them to retreat—they struggled with fever, blindness, and the common ailments of age. Many of them suffered periods of utter despair and loneliness in their pursuit of what they knew was right and true.

Lorraine Hansberry, author of *Raisin in the Sun*, wrote, "The thing that makes you exceptional, if you are at all, is inevitably that which must also make you lonely."[1]

How true. For each of these women, their individual passions were not always understood by friends, family, and society. What they most wanted to achieve, others considered ridiculous, impossible, or worthless.

Yet, through it all, when others shuddered, these women refused to give up.

The stories in this book focus on women who lived from the late 1800s to the early 1900s. This was a time of significant change in the United States. The woman's role in the home and society was shifting as women, collectively, began to achieve a greater voice. This changing role for women also impacted the church. Women began to want to do more, to serve in more daring ways, to have a noble purpose, to achieve things for God that reached beyond the sphere of their home.

The thing that makes you exceptional, if you are at all, is inevitably that which must also make you lonely.

My search for stories began with one woman in particular. As a graduate of Moody Bible Institute, I had often heard it said that a woman named Emma Dryer should receive at least partial credit for the founding of the school.

Moody Bible Institute began in the late 1800s. Just before the Chicago fire, Moody invited a young single schoolteacher named Emma Dryer to help with his Bible work in Chicago—a city that was young, vibrant, and growing. I wanted to know more about Emma's story. Why did she come to Chicago? How did she meet D. L. Moody? What role did she play in the founding of this college?

So, I reached into the past, digging through boxes of archives, fragile letters, and diary entries to learn a bit more about these eight women . . . women who came to the urban centers of our country, who worked alongside the church and men like D. L. Moody, who believed in God and thought they could help change the world for His glory.

I have tried to tell each woman's story with accurate historic detail taken, as much as possible, from her own words or the words of those who knew her best. I wanted my readers to hear, firsthand, the personal memories that had shaped each woman's life, faith, and work. In each case, the opening narrative is based upon fact, but the exact scene and dialogue is fictionalized to bring it to life for my reader. I wanted people to not just learn historical detail, but to walk with each woman through her struggles and triumphs. These are certainly not exhaustive records of their achievements. Instead, I have attempted to give glimpses into the moments that made each of their lives memorable.

Many times, during my research, I would stop reading a journal or letter and set it down as tears filled my eyes. I would shake my head and wonder, "How did she do it?" "How did she keep going?"

And then, inevitably, I would say to myself, "God, I want to be like that."

What I discovered has amazed and impressed me deeply. In many ways, these women were ordinary—just like you and me. Some were lucky in love, others remained single (by choice or not). Some were highly educated, others only had a few months of schooling, but each of them was driven by a heartfelt desire to serve God well. They wanted their lives to count for something more and were increasingly dissatisfied with society's ideal of a "proper" woman.

They refused to be stereotyped. They were tireless and persistent. They pushed past boundaries and faced obstacles fearlessly. They were patient and faithful and worked alongside men—some who supported them and others who did not. They walked into neighborhoods and communities where others feared to tread. They were completely devoted to God and clearly communicated His Word to a world they felt desperately needed it.

The more I read, the more their lives inspired my own.

As I walk the streets of Chicago today, I think about those days, more than 100 years ago, when Emma, Fanny, Nettie, Mary, Sarah, Virginia, Amanda, and Evangeline laced their boots, lifted their long skirts, and walked to work.

They were tireless.

They were fierce.

They persisted.

They believed.

No matter what the obstacle—they refused to give up.

I do not think these women knew they were leaving behind a great legacy. They did not consider their work brave, courageous, extraordinary, or world-changing. They just did what was set before them. They fed the poor. They preached the gospel. They taught children. What they did not realize was that the organizations they began, the hymns they wrote, the words they spoke, left a long-lasting legacy. Many of the organizations that they worked so hard to begin still thrive today.

They changed history.

These are their stories. It is my hope that the details of their lives will encourage and challenge your own life today. I hope that through learning about these women who have gone before, that you will realize how God is using *your* ordinary life in amazing ways, to make a difference for eternity.

FANNY CROSBY

1820–1915

CHAPTER ONE

Longings of a Blind Girl

Fanny sat next to her grandmother Eunice on the old, wooden rocking chair. It was her place of safety and comfort. She fingered the hem of her grandmother's worn cotton apron and nestled closer to her soft, warm body, listening to the words of Scripture. Her grandmother's voice was kind and firm. No matter how long she would read, Fanny always asked for just a bit more.

"It's a beautiful day, Fanny," said her grandmother, reaching for her cane and straightening her aging knees. "Let's go for a little walk."

Taking the child's hand in her own, she led Fanny off the porch and down the path. Guiding her carefully over the stony ground, she described the blossoms on a nearby apple tree. "It won't be long," she said, "and we will see apples on this tree—shiny red and shaped like a tooth."

"A tooth," said Fanny, laughing. "That's a funny shape!" She loved these nature walks—just the two of them—where she could touch and feel and smell the nature objects with her grandma. She could almost glimpse the golden sunlight, but the rest was just a shadow. Frances Jane Crosby had been blind since she was an infant.

She was born March 24, 1820, in eastern Putnam County of New York. Frances, or "Fanny" as she was called, was the only child of John and Mercy Crosby. Fanny never knew her father as she was only one year old when he died. She was raised among women: her mother and grandmother, as well as extended family. The Crosbys came from Puritan stock—with a solid Christian faith and a strong, serious work ethic.

Fanny did not remember when she became blind. As her mother explained, it happened when she was just six weeks old. Mercy was worried about her infant daughter who had developed a severe cold—the baby's eyes were inflamed and red. Since the family doctor was out of town, they asked another self-proclaimed medical expert, traveling through the area, for assistance. The stranger applied a hot mustard poultice to little Fanny's eyes. While the poultice might have helped reduce the swelling, it also burned and left the little girl completely blind. The man left shortly after the incident and was never heard from again.

Throughout her life, Fanny said she never felt a spark of resentment against the man. When Fanny was in her late eighties, she wrote: "I have always believed from my youth to this very moment that the good Lord, in His infinite Mercy, by this means consecrated me to the work that I am permitted to do."[1]

Although she was blind and the world darkened around her, Fanny describes a childhood filled with sunshine and happiness. She never wanted her blindness to cause others to treat her differently. She was full of energy and mischief—and loved to play with the other children in town.

Fanny said, "One of the earliest resolves that I formed in my young and joyous heart was to leave all care to yesterday and believe that the morrow would bring forth its own peculiar joy, and behold, when the morrow dawns, I generally have found that the human spirit can take on the rosy tints of the reddening east."[2]

Fanny was taught plain language by the Quakers and Scripture from her grandmother. She was determined to learn as much as she could and refused to be limited by her blindness. "Why should the blind be regarded as objects of pity?" said Fanny.[3]

While Fanny had an optimistic attitude, her mother, Mercy, struggled with the unfairness of her daughter's infirmity. Why should her little girl have this terrible disability? Why should she live in a world shrouded in darkness? As a mother, she felt pressure to do something, to find a solution, to solve the problem. She talked to doctors, seeking medical advice, and was finally referred to a famous physician in New York City, Dr. Valentine Mott—the best eye specialist in the United States of America. If anyone could cure Fanny's blindness, it was Dr. Mott. Mercy was excited and determined to meet him.

She and Fanny, then just five years old, traveled to New York by horse drawn carriage and boat. Mercy became ill on the sea voyage and left Fanny in the care of the captain who entertained the little girl by telling "sea yarns."

Fanny remembers sitting on the deck of the boat and having tea. It was April, and the sun was setting. Although most of the beauty was invisible to her, she could distinguish some faint colors on the right kinds of background. Today, she could see a faint golden hue from the blinding sunset. "I sat there on the deck, amid the glories of departing day, the low murmur of the waves soothed my soul into delightful peace."[4]

Once they finally reached their destination, the doctor's visit was disappointing. Dr. Mott, after careful examination, confirmed what Mercy probably suspected was true. With great sadness, the doctor delivered the bad news—Fanny would never recover her eyesight. This was devastating to Mercy who had set great hopes upon the doctor. The return trip was somber. This time it was Mercy who turned to the comfort of her own mother for words of hope from hymns and Scripture.

While others were devastated by a lack of cures for the little girl's condition, Fanny refused to be seen as an object of pity. She wrote this poem at age eight:

"Oh, what a happy soul I am,
Although I cannot see,
I am resolved that in this world
Contented I will be.

How many blessings I enjoy
That other people don't!
To weep and sigh because I'm blind
I cannot and I won't."[5]

Her childhood was a normal one, or as normal as it could be without the ability to see. Fanny wrote later, "The sunny hours of my childhood flowed onwardly as placidly as the waters of the Hudson."[6] She would attend the village school from time to time, but the teacher was often too busy with the other children to spend time individually with young Fanny.

The little girl had discovered, much to the amazement of her family and teacher, that she was a bit of a poet. She could weave together bits of verse and begged her mom to read her famous poems. She loved words and music. Twice a week, she took singing lessons from a traveling music teacher who would visit their church. As she sat with the other children on the hard wooden pews of the old Presbyterian meeting house, the room would echo with the joyful strains of Handel and Haydn.

Fanny loved to read stories. She heard about the adventures of Robin Hood and Don Quixote. She was raised on Sunday school stories and easily memorized the Bible. "Many quiet evenings, I would sit alone in the twilight and repeat all the poems and passages of Scripture I knew."[7]

She was smart and hungry for more. Her grandmother did all she could to satisfy Fanny's growing desire for knowledge, but it was often not enough. Fanny said it felt like a great barrier rising before her shutting her out from the information she so desired. In the quiet hours of the evening, when no one had time to entertain her, she would often pray to God, "Dear Lord, please show me how I can learn like other children."

Her blindness, while she did not see it as a limitation, did restrict her abilities to learn the way she desired. She could not attend school each day like the other children. She could not read books on her own. She was always dependent on the kindness and patience of others to satisfy her growing craving for knowledge. Fanny wrote: "I was not content always to live in ignorance, and, in the course of time, in a way of which I had no previous intimation, my wish was to be granted in fullest measure."[8]

One day, in November of 1834, an acquaintance told Mercy Crosby about a new school in New York City—a school specifically intended to educate the blind. Mercy was conflicted by the news. How could she send her daughter so far away? How would she protect her? How could she bear the separation from the little girl she loved so dearly? Yet, she knew that this would be an amazing opportunity for her daughter.

Somewhat reluctantly, she told Fanny about the New York Institution for the Blind. "It was the happiest day of my life," said Fanny. "Not that I craved physical vision—for it was mental enlightenment that I sought. It was my star of promise."[9]

Certainly a few tears were shed while mother and grandmother packed clean clothing and supplies for young Fanny's journey. Finally, the trunk was shut with a resounding click, and all that was left was to bid farewell to their girl.

On March 3, 1835, a stagecoach pulled to the door of the Crosby home. Fanny hugged her mother closely, and trembled a bit as she was pulled into the familiar arms of her grandmother. She almost turned around and went back into the safety of her home. Her mouth felt dry and her stomach rumbled with nervousness.

Could she leave behind everything she had ever known? Taking the hand of the stagecoach driver, she stepped up and took her seat. She could not see her mother or grandmother waving as the coach pulled away from her childhood home, but she knew exactly what they looked like.

Tears silently fell down the young girl's face—and she fumbled for her handkerchief to wipe them away. She refused to look sad. She knew this was the right decision. It was what she had longed for—it was what she had prayed for year after year. "Please God, be my vision," Fanny prayed. "Thank You for answering my prayers. Help me to have the courage to follow Your leading."

The stagecoach, carrying Fanny and other passengers, rumbled toward the bustling, growing metropolis of New York City.

CHAPTER TWO

Learning and Love

A s the stagecoach pulled up to the New York Institution for the Blind, Fanny felt as if her heart was beating loudly enough for everyone to hear. She was nervous, yes, but also terribly excited. A fellow traveler asked her if this school was her destination.

"Yes," said the young girl. "Can you tell me what it looks like?"

The school resembled a large European castle. It stood three stories tall with elaborate stone turrets—four rising in the center over the doorways. Surrounding the building were acres of grass and trees and a lovely view of the Hudson River.

The New York Institution for the Blind was founded by several men who believed the blind could be educated. Up until that point, those struck blind, deaf, or dumb were pitied but were not believed to be useful members of society. The New York Institution for the Blind opened in 1832, just three years before Fanny arrived. The school started simply, in a single room in lower Manhattan, but soon moved to the grand estate donated by James Boorman.[10]

On that first day, Fanny was taken to the little room where she would sleep. Someone brought in her trunk, and as she sat on the bed, she thought how strange it all seemed. She did not know anyone at the school. No one knew her. She felt utterly alone.

Although she was determined to be brave, when the matron arrived to check on her new student, Fanny broke down in tears. The Quaker woman drew the small girl into her arms, hugged her, and let her cry. It was frightening to begin a new life, and to be so far away from home.[11]

Fanny's sadness did not last for long. She was warmly welcomed to the school by the superintendent, Dr. John Ross, and became their thirty-fifth pupil. "I loved him dearly," wrote Fanny at a later time.[12] She was excited to begin her studies. With her fellow students, she was taught Scripture and poetry and learned a phonetic alphabet. The students learned by reading and lecture, as Braille had not yet been invented. The school was very strict, and no conversations were allowed between boys and girls. However, Fanny jokes, "I was one of the first to revolt."[13]

As much as Fanny loved literature, she despised mathematics. "I loathe, abhor, it makes me sick / to hear the word, Arithmetic!" quipped the young girl, framing her thoughts in her best talent, poetry.[14] Fanny's gift for writing, music, and poetry quickly became obvious to both her teachers and fellow pupils during her years at the school.

She wrote so many poems that one day she was called in to the principal's office. Fanny was certain she was being commissioned to write for a special occasion. Instead, she was reprimanded for becoming too prideful about her talent. The schoolmaster told her, "We have no right to be vain in the presence of the Owner and Creator of all things."[15] From then on, Fanny determined to give God the credit for her abilities.

One day, a phrenologist visited the school to examine all of the pupils. Phrenology was a medical and scientific fad at that time—studying the shape and measurements of the skull to determine personality and ability. After closely examining the shape of Fanny's skull, the expert declared that "This young lady is a born poetess. She should be encouraged."[16]

When Fanny was twenty-two, after attending the school for seven years, she was appointed as a teacher. She would instruct students in the areas of rhetoric and history.[17] Fanny was thrilled and honored by this new position. She loved learning, loved young people, and enjoyed this confirmation of her intelligence. This also gave her a platform to meet others. Since the school was considered highly innovative, many famous people would come to visit and observe the "new" methods of education.

Fanny, because of her charm and outgoing nature, was often asked to greet the guests—and, sometimes, to recite one of her poems. Among the many famous visitors Fanny met during those years were: singer Jenny Lind (the "Swedish Nightingale"); the United States 11th president, James Polk; poet and journalist William Cullen Bryant; and publisher Horace Greeley. She was thrilled when the publisher invited her to write poems for his New York paper, the *Tribune*.

Interest in the school and in blind education continued to grow, and the next year, 1834, Fanny was invited to speak before the United States Congress with a delegation of students and faculty from the New York Institution. Fanny wrote an original poem for the event. Normally, she had no problem reading her poems, but the prospect of speaking before such a large and prestigious audience made her extremely nervous. She prayed to God to help her as she spoke: "I believe I have never refused to pray or speak in a public service, with the result that I have been richly blessed."[18]

The audience, a joint assembly of both houses, was moved to tears by the young blind poetess who wrote such beautiful poetry and recited so confidently. Throughout the years, Fanny's political ties continued, and she became friends with several presidents, most closely with President Grover Cleveland. Before he became president of the United States, Cleveland served alongside Fanny as a faculty member at the school. "To know and make friends with the builders of this nation was a desire of my growing womanhood," said Fanny.[19]

Many years later, after a lifetime of friendship, Cleveland wrote of Fanny, "It is more than fifty years ago that our acquaintance and friendship began, and ever since that time I have watched your continuous and disinterested labor in uplifting humanity and pointing out the way to an appreciation of God's goodness and mercy."[20]

In 1844, Fanny published her first collection of poetry, *The Blind Girl, and Other Poems*. Her life was happy and full. As a teacher and a writer, she was traveling and speaking. She was expanding her mind and heart in ways she had never thought possible as a girl. And then, her life expanded in a way she had never dared to hope: Fanny fell deeply and madly in love.

Alexander Van Alstyne came to the Institute in the 1840s as one of Fanny's students. He had been stricken blind just a few years earlier, and his mother sought out Fanny to instruct her son. Alexander, or "Van" as Fanny called him, was described as magnetic and charming.[21] Students at the school were not grouped according to age and many came to the Institution at various points in their life. Van was an older student.

He shared her love of music and literature—and was also a theologian and philosopher. In 1855, he was asked to continue on at the school as an instructor, and their friendship deepened. Fanny said, "After hearing several of my poems, he became deeply interested."[22]

"One day in June he went out under the elm trees to listen to the birds sing, and the winds play their love-song among the leaves. It was here the voice of love spoke," recalled Fanny of the moment the two fell in love. "I placed my right hand on his left and called him 'Van.'" [23]

In 1858, the two were married. This drew concern from faculty and family who did not see how two blind people could manage a relationship. But Fanny had fallen in love—and this is what she wanted. Both Van and Fanny resigned from their faculty positions and left the school to begin their married life together. Van accepted a position as a teacher of music and a church organist. He was a composer and would often collaborate with his wife. One project that they both enjoyed was writing hymns for children's Sunday school.[24]

Despite their best intentions, their married life was not ideal. Being blind, they often boarded with others and had little privacy. Also, during the early years of their marriage, Fanny gave birth to their first and only child. The child died shortly afterward. Fanny rarely spoke of the deeply personal loss. She wrote, in one autobiography: "Now I am going to tell you of something that only my closest friends know. I became a mother and knew a mother's love. God gave us a tender babe but the angels came down and took our infant up to God and to His throne."[25]

Fanny and Van led rather separate lives. Fanny retained her own name, at Van's insistence, to preserve her growing identity as a poetess and hymn writer. The relationship, which had started out as a romantic one, became more of a companionship and remained stressed for decades.[26] Later in life, they moved into separate homes.

One biographer wrote, "As a young woman, Crosby had longed for romantic love. At age thirty-eight, she thought she had found it with Van. The rift in their relationship had left this daughter of primitive Presbyterians the option to interpret her failure to realize a loving marriage as a discipline God sent for her good." [27]

While the couple did not appear to share a romantic relationship, they did have a collegial one. Even after separating, they worked together often on musical compositions, and Fanny always spoke highly of Van. She wrote once, "He had his faults—and so have I mine. But, notwithstanding these, we loved each other to the last." In one of her poems, written shortly after Van's death at age seventy, she penned these words: "And tho, at times the things I ask / In love are oft denied, / I know he gives me what is best, / and I am satisfied."[28]

At age fifteen, Fanny had left behind her childhood home to seek education. Then, at age thirty-eight, she left her teaching and school to find love. What would be next? Now in her forties, her life was again in a time of transition. How she wished she could "see" what waited for her around the next corner.

CHAPTER THREE

Hymns and Heaven

❦

I t was a hot and sweaty evening in New York. The August night felt thick and close as she entered the doors of the Manhattan rescue mission. In addition to her work in music and hymn writing, Fanny devoted a great deal of her time to serving at New York's rescue missions. Tonight, she was attending the evening service of the Bowery Mission.[29]

The room was filled to capacity. The city of New York had experienced a huge swell of immigrants. Religious institutions, like the Bowery, were among the first to fill those needs through the services of a mission, opening their doors to the misfortunate.

As Fanny entered, she could feel the warm breeze of people waving paper programs. She could hear people shuffling as they took their seats and the strong scent of unwashed clothing hung in the air. As she prayed for God's blessing on those who attended, a thought kept pressing on her heart. She was convinced that someone sitting in the room needed God's love and forgiveness.

Following the sermon, Fanny rose to her feet and invited "any boy who had wandered away from his mother's teaching" to stay and talk with her. In a few moments, an eighteen-year-old boy came and sat beside her. When she heard his story, she prayed for him. The young man said, "Now, I can meet my mother in heaven; for I have found her God."[30]

Fanny went home, and the next day the idea began twisting and turning in her mind. She would compose her hymns without paper by repeating phrases and key words, forming and reshaping lines to convey meaning in a beautiful way. These words came to her that evening:

"Rescue the perishing, care for the dying.
Snatch them in pity from sin and the grave;
Weep o'er the erring one, lift up the fallen,
Tell them of Jesus, the Mighty to Save."

And then, she penned the beautiful words of the chorus:

"Rescue the perishing, care for the dying!
Jesus is merciful. Jesus will save."[31]

"Rescue the Perishing" became one of Fanny's most well-known hymns. Thirty-five years later, Fanny would meet that young man again—at a gospel meeting in Massachusetts. "I am the man you prayed with that night," he would tell the small woman whose forthright manner had changed the course of his life. "I sought and found peace."[32]

In the years following her marriage, Fanny's career in hymn writing gained speed. At age forty-four, she felt like she had at last discovered her life's true purpose. To write a hymn, she would begin with prayer. Sometimes, after listening to a tune, the words would come quickly. Other times, she would edit the lines in her mind, always holding a notebook in her hand (although she could not see it and never wrote anything down). She said, "It has been my custom to hold a little book in my hand; and somehow or other the words seem to come more promptly when I am so engaged."[33] Fanny was prolific, sometimes writing as many as seven hymns a day— even composing two hymns at once, alternating lines.

Small events would trigger new poems. One day, while sitting in her room thinking about God's blessings in her life, a friend came to pay a visit. As he left, he gave her ten dollars. The gift, completely unexpected, became a poem in her mind. The words of "All the Way My Savior Leads Me" were formed from that experience. Fanny once said, "The most enduring hymns are born in the silence of the soul, and nothing must be allowed to intrude while they are being framed into language."[34]

As her career grew, Fanny worked closely with many male musicians to create the hymns. As one biographer noted, her blindness might have provided a way to break through the gender barriers of her time and to spend time collaborating, often alone, with talented men.[35]

Two of the people who were among her most frequent collaborators were millionaires: William Howard Doane and Phoebe Palmer Knapp. Doane had made his fortune in industry in quickly growing Chicago. He gave much of his growing fortune to religious institutions.[36] Although he was a successful businessman, his true love was music, specifically church music. As he worked, he would often hum and whistle tunes, composing music even as he earned a wage at other tasks.

Fanny initiated the meeting with Doane in the spring of 1867. She had written a new poem and had a messenger carry it to him. It came at an opportune moment, for Doane had been asked to supply a new hymn for the anniversary of a rescue mission. The messenger handed him Crosby's text: "More like Jesus would I be, Let my Savior dwell in me . . ." Doane knew the words were special. He found Crosby in her room in lower Manhattan and told her that God had brought them together.

Fanny also enjoyed a working relationship with the wealthy Phoebe Palmer Knapp. Fanny and Phoebe attended the same church and composed many hymns together. One day, Phoebe sent one of her tunes to Fanny in need of words. In 1873, the now famous hymn "Blessed Assurance" was born.[37]

Although Fanny was working with men and women of great affluence, she never assumed airs of importance herself. The tiny woman was known to live simply and to frequent undesirable areas of town, helping in rescue homes for prostitutes, drunks, and thieves. Much like she had expressed as a young girl, she wanted her life to be useful. She looked forward to her visits as an opportunity to do good, and her experiences lent a grittiness and reality to her hymn writing.

In the 1870s, Fanny became acquainted with two men. Evangelist Dwight L. Moody and his musical partner, Ira D. Sankey, were arriving in New York for evangelistic meetings. Together, they would make Fanny Crosby and her heartfelt hymns a household name.

> *Suffering is no argument for God's Displeasure but a part of the fiber of our lives.*

In 1876, Moody had returned to New York for a second series of evangelistic meetings. Crowds had gathered at P. T. Barnum's Hippodrome, an 8,000-seat auditorium, to hear the famed evangelist. A choir of 1,250 voices was rehearsing for the evening's meeting. Sankey planned to introduce a new hymn to New York City—"Rescue the Perishing" written by Fanny Crosby.[38] The hymn became so popular that it spread across America and to many countries of the world.

Fanny's work with Sankey continued, and she wrote an estimated 8,000 hymns under as many as 200 pseudonyms.[39] So great was the demand for her work that publishers feared her name would get overused. Sankey and Crosby remained lifelong friends. Almost every one of her hymns focused on the anticipation of heaven. Her lyrics saw her future eternal home as a place of peace, joy, and rest. In 1899, when her good friend D. L. Moody died, she knew another soul was now waiting for her on the other side.

In July of 1902, while visiting the home of friends, a telegram brought tragic news. Her husband, Van, had died. Although the couple had been living separately, the news was devastating to Fanny. She went into her bedroom and closed the door. Several hours later she emerged with a new hymn expressing her sorrow and also her reconciliation to the relationship that was never quite what she had hoped it would be. Each line ended with the words, "I am satisfied."[40]

Fanny continued to be active in hymn writing and social work through her eighties. At the age of ninety-one, Crosby made her final appearance at an evangelistic tent meeting in Manhattan. Five thousand people came to hear the small woman speak. "When I came in and you greeted me so warmly, I wanted to weep tears of joy," said Fanny. One newspaper reported that the audience thought she would be frail and feeble. She told them "When I was taken from the carriage into the hotel today, I heard someone say, 'Get her a rolling chair.' But I spoke right up and said, 'I don't need any rolling chair. I can walk on my own feet. My strength is from the Lord.'"[41]

She continued to be spirited and positive in her final years. She wrote, "I have been careful of cultivating a sunny disposition. . . . I made up my mind years ago that I would never become a disagreeable old woman."[42] She refused to let her blindness, or the trials of life result in a negative perspective. She said, "Suffering is no argument for God's displeasure but a part of the fiber of our lives."[43]

I do not know but that on the whole it has been a good thing that I have been blind. How in the world could I have lived such a helpful life as I have, were it not that I am blind. I am very well satisfied.

At age ninety-two, Fanny was taken in a great parade down the streets of Cambridge, Massachusetts, while a band played her beloved hymn, "Rescue the Perishing." She had certainly become well loved, a "saint in behalf of humanity."[44]

In February of 1915, Fanny suffered a massive stroke and died. Her niece, who was with her at the time, wrote, "I am lonesome, for she was both my care and my comfort. But I know she is safely home. What a meeting she must have had with all gone before when—as she said so many times—the first her eyes would behold would be Jesus."[45]

Friend Eliza Hewitt sent a poem to be read at her funeral: "Our song bird has taken her flight; And she who had sung in the darkness so long, Now sings in the beautiful light."[46] Mourners sent armloads of Fanny's favorite flower, the violet.

Her obituary, published in the *New York Times,* said, "Throughout her life Miss Crosby's cheerful spirit was unaffected by her affliction. She once said: 'I do not know but that on the whole it has been a good thing that I have been blind. How in the world could I have lived such a helpful life as I have, were it not that I am blind. I am very well satisfied.'"[47]

One time a Scottish evangelist asked her: "Miss Crosby, I think it is a great pity that the good Master, when he showered so many gifts upon you, did not give you sight."

Fanny answered, "Do you know that if at my birth I had been able to make one petition to my Creator it would have been that I should be made blind."

The evangelist was startled. "Why?" he asked.

"Because," said Fanny, "when I get to heaven, the first face that shall ever gladden my sight will be that of my Savior."[48]

"EMMA" EMELINE E. DRYER

1835–1925

CHAPTER FOUR

Typhoid Fever and God's Call to Service

E mma felt as if she was being burned alive.

The thirty-five-year-old pushed back the quilts that were piled high and weighed heavily upon her frail body. Her bedclothes were soaked with sweat. Her lips were dry and cracked. The schoolmistress knew she should get up, grade papers, go to her faculty office, but she was unable to even lift her head from the pillow.

For the past three weeks, she had been afflicted with typhoid fever, a disease that had already killed thousands of Americans in the mid-1800s. The bacterial infection had spread quickly throughout her body, beginning with a dull stomachache and followed by a rising fever. For three weeks, her temperature had hovered at 104 degrees, and she was unable to keep any food down.

The visiting doctor had prescribed complete bed rest, a difficult task for the determined woman who had worked all of her life. A neighbor, in the house where she boarded, would knock on her door to check on her from time to time, but Emma felt utterly alone. Never had the hours seemed to pass more slowly.

Emma's room was quiet, except for the steady ticking of the mantel clock. She was unable even to lift her head to check the time, knowing only that the shadows of the room shifted each time she awakened. Sips of weak broth or tea, left on her bedside table, were all that sustained her, and she closed her eyes, trying to whisper a prayer, asking God to spare her life.

"God help me," she murmured, willing herself not to give in to the pain and delirium. The fever was too strong, she was too tired, and she wanted to give up.

As she hovered between consciousness and sleep, Emma found comfort in reciting the Bible verses of her youth. "The Lord is my shepherd, I shall not want"(Psalm 23:1), she whispered through parched, dry lips.

"My grace is sufficient for thee" (2 Corinthians 12:9).

"Blessed be the name of the Lord" (Psalm 113:2).

These were the words that brought the greatest comfort to her soul, the Bible verses that had been taught to her since childhood. Emeline Dryer was born in Massachusetts in 1835. The daughter of John and Lucinda Dryer of Victor, New York, Emma was brought up in the church and with a solid knowledge of the Scriptures.[1] Emma was used to hard work and took her studies seriously. Like most children in the East Coast region of the United States, she attended the local primary school, but, for Emma, that brief taste of education was not enough. She wanted so much more.

Emma decided to pursue additional schooling. She was a thinker, a dreamer, a girl who wanted more out of life. She was easily bored by housework—always had her nose in the books. Because she was an excellent student, her family provided the way for her to continue her education.

Although many people feared that additional schooling would make women unfit for marriage and motherhood, Emma enrolled in one of the earliest women's schools in the United States, Ingham University, then called the LeRoy Female Seminary. Founded by two female missionaries, the seminary was the high school of its time, taking female students one step closer toward advancing their educational goals.[2]

Never had Emma been surrounded by so many women who loved to learn. She enjoyed living in the boardinghouse with the other girls. The school championed the arts, and boasted a conservatory, gallery, and studios. The love of learning at LeRoy infected Emma's mind and her heart. She applied herself to her work and excelled, graduating in 1858 with highest honors. For two years, she remained on at LeRoy teaching astronomy and mathematics.[3]

Emma believed that if anything was to be done at all, it should be done with excellence. She found that she not only loved being a student, but that she excelled as a teacher. Her quick mind and attention to detail earned her a position on the teaching faculty of the Ewing Female University in Knoxville, Illinois.[4]

Teaching jobs were popular for women in the northern United States. Since Southern women did not find such work fashionable, women from the North were quick to fill the positions. During these years, the Civil War had erupted between the North and the South. From 1861 to 1865, life became increasingly challenging. The war separated men from families, destroyed properties, and made traveling conditions difficult.[5]

As the war neared its end, in 1864 Emma left Knoxville for Illinois State Normal University, where she became a "preceptress," or head instructor, at the age of twenty-nine. The training school for teachers was in a setting unlike her home in the East Coast. Surrounded by farms, the fields seemed to reach on forever. Winds gusted across the rural campus, making walking in the long billowing skirts of the day difficult at best. One year after she arrived, the "normal" school—a university dedicated to teacher education—moved to the neighboring town of Normal, Illinois, where a new campus was being built.

Emma knew her choices in life had been unusual. Even with her secure salary and prestigious ranking at the university, she sometimes wondered if grading piles of papers and preparing lectures were all that the future held for her. Relatives from back East often sent word of the most recent marriages and the birth of children. No one asked whether or not she would marry. They assumed the decision had been made.

Popular opinion dictated that girls who went to college would likely be "old maids" and become "bookworms." This was considered a dire threat to any girl's chance of attracting a husband. Indeed, Emma had chosen a different path. She sometimes felt alone in the world, an independent spirit whose only children would be her students and whose lifelong goal was to make the world a better place through education.

While the United States was facing a bitter Civil War, Emma devoted herself to her teaching career. She loved the orderliness of her work as a teacher of grammar and drawing. She enjoyed the eagerness of her students, their faces fixed on her or knotted in concentration as they completed their lessons and examinations. She enjoyed preparing lectures and even grading papers, correcting their mistakes, urging her students to be more exacting in their work.

Of course, there were hours when she wondered if there were more to her life than being a single teacher. Would she end her days alone in a boardinghouse, with only her students for company? What about her childhood dreams of travel and foreign missionary work? She felt so burdened for the need for Christian work even among the women of her own country. How was she, Emma Dryer, meant to serve God? As a teacher, certainly. But was there more?

As she lay in her sickbed, unaccustomed as she was to inactivity, memories flooded her troubled mind and heart. She continued to cry out to God, for healing from this terrible illness, for a second chance at life, for the opportunity to serve Him more deliberately. She was prepared to die, and she began to think that the end was indeed near. She would meet God, enter His holy gates with rejoicing. Her time to leave this world, perhaps, had come.

At last, Emma fell into a fitful sleep. Hours passed, with concerned friends and neighbors standing vigil by her bedside. When she at last woke from her delirium, the fever had finally broken. She distinctly felt the healing power of God, and knew, without any doubt, that her prayers for healing had been answered.

She propped herself up in the bed, pushed back the heavy blankets, and peered at the calendar. It had been almost four weeks since she had fallen ill. Now she felt only impatience and a restlessness to get up and move forward. There was so much to do! Although she was still quite weak, her mind, at last, was clear.

"I saw the needs of this dying world, as never before, especially the fallen, wretched condition of the masses around me."

Emma Dryer knew God had saved her life. He had healed her for a purpose. She wrote in her memoirs, "I saw the needs of this dying world, as never before, especially the fallen, wretched condition of the masses around me."[6]

Emma did not know then, the mighty ways that God would use her, or to where she would be called. But she had no doubt that God had spared her life for a divine purpose. God had shown her, in her utter weakness, that He had created her for a purpose—even bigger than she would ever have imagined.

Her life had echoed the Scriptures, as she saw God's will most clearly when her own abilities had failed. It called to mind the verse that had come to her during her time of illness, 2 Corinthians 12:9: "My grace is sufficient for thee: for my strength is made perfect in weakness. Most gladly therefore will I rather glory in my infirmities, that the power of Christ may rest upon me."

It would be in the bustling urban city of Chicago, miles away from rural Normal, Illinois, where she would discover her calling.

CHAPTER FIVE

The Chicago Fire Brings a Fresh Start

◦──────⸎⸎❦⸎⸎──────◦

S till recovering from her near death from typhoid fever, Emma spent a good portion of the summer of 1870 staying with friends in Chicago. In the city, she experienced a bit of culture shock—trading the cornfields of Illinois for the bustle of the quickly growing industrial center. Chicago, in just ten years, had exploded in population, increasing from 100,000 to nearly 300,000 residents. Some said it was the fastest growing city in the Western world.[7]

The city's streets were teeming with horses and buggies. Buildings climbed skyward. But the grandeur of the architecture was balanced by the inability of the city to keep up with its growing numbers. Streets were filled with waste as the city struggled to maintain adequate sanitation. More people arrived each day by train and carriage in hopes of finding work in the city's steel mills, factories, and stockyards. Single women were among the hopeful workers, although many of them were lured into houses of prostitution on the city's notorious South Side. Poverty faced immigrant families who struggled to clothe their children and keep food on their tables.

With the growing population in Chicago came more and more opportunities for Christian work. These circumstances, facing her at every corner, echoed the call that Emma had so strongly felt during her illness. The thirty-five-year-old was torn. Should she return to Normal, Illinois, and continue her teaching career at Illinois State University or move to Chicago to work among the poor and needy of the great city?

She was finding her heart pulled toward the many "wayward" women who had arrived in Chicago. Like her, these women were often unmarried. But they often made unwise choices and lived far from God. Some of them became pregnant and many had taken work as prostitutes or bar maids. Emma felt God speaking to her once again, urging her to give up her life of solitude and safety and extend her hand to those in need of His love and redemption.[8]

> *Emma felt God speaking to her once again, urging her to give up her life of solitude and safety and extend her hand to those in need of His love and redemption.*

Emma was becoming more and more serious about both Bible study and Christian service. "The Bible became a new book. God's plans were not experiments," wrote Emma. "His Word never failed."[9] During this time she was introduced to teachings about the imminent return of Christ. This meant that the Lord's return could come at any moment. It renewed her resolve to reach out to a world in need.[10]

She had seen God's work in her own life, and she knew He would continue to guide her no matter what the future held. Emma also believed the Bible was the solution to the social problems she saw in Chicago. Her intent was to get a Bible into the hands of every woman in the city and to train them to lead Bible studies of their own.[11] She wanted to show women how to lead devotional discussions with their families. She began to organize a group of Christian women who shared her concerns. They planned to contact every resident in the city and began working on organizing educational centers for Bible training.

That summer, she was staying at the home of Mr. and Mrs. Daniels, a pastor and his wife who were her very good friends. As she gradually regained her strength, she began attending church services at the Illinois Street Church founded by the renowned evangelist D. L. Moody. Her friends told her that Mr. Moody had asked about her. She couldn't imagine why the famous evangelist would inquire about her![12]

Like herself, Moody was originally from the East Coast. He had come to Chicago in the 1850s, drawn by the word of revival and the desperate needs of the urban poor, particularly the street children. Moody soon started a Sunday school to reach the "poorest of the poor."[13] He helped organize the Chicago YMCA and entered full-time ministry in 1860. His ministry in Chicago had flourished. The small Sunday school had grown to attract nearly a thousand children and teens and as many as three hundred adults. Moody started the Illinois Street Church in December of 1864.[14] Although he had been heavily involved in travel, both in the United States and England, Moody and his wife continually returned home to Chicago where his church continued to flourish.

Later that summer, she finally met with Mr. Moody and learned more about his work and vision for ministry. The straight-talking Moody intrigued Emma. "I liked his Christian earnestness," she said. "His direct way of introducing a subject and reaching its most important truth."[15]

Despite her determination to serve God, she was still struggling with her health. Later that fall, while feeling poorly, she stayed overnight at the home of her friends the Eberharts.[16] The weather that day was warm and windy—the city had been under a severe drought, and the local firemen were tired from fighting small scattered fires that kept popping up around the city.

On the night of October 8, 1871, the Great Chicago Fire began. The sight of the flames spreading as far north and south as they could see was both terrifying and awesome. Emma joined her friends at the window where they could watch the blaze coming ever closer. "We saw a veering wind, fearing that the fire might be blown one more point westward, and so destroy the entire city," wrote Emma.[17] The wind held its northward course and the river helped spare the west side of the city. The devastation, however, was widespread.

Among the city's 300,000 population, as many as 100,000 residents were left homeless by the great fire. Of these, many were the poorest immigrants, already barely able to meet their families' basic needs before the tragedy. The area of destruction spread four miles long and nearly one mile wide. One hundred and twenty-five people were confirmed dead—although some thought as many as 300 had perished in the blaze and smoke. The fire raged for three days, finally subsiding only when the heavens opened and a heavy rain fell upon the charred, blackened ruins that had once been Chicago.[18]

Many people, including Emma Dryer, lost everything in the Chicago fire. "Every article of clothing except what I was wearing at the time was burned in the fire," she wrote.[19] Emma's home, her books, and her belongings were completely destroyed. Her life, however, was spared.

Rather than being discouraged by the tragedy, the resolute schoolteacher felt a confirmation of God's call upon her life and immediately headed to work. Chicago's mayor called together all the women who were available to help. They met at a church on the west side of the city and began to organize the task ahead.[20]

"We were all at once busy, ministering to the homeless, the sick and the suffering," wrote Emma. With her leadership, the YWCA reorganized itself, temporarily, as the Chicago Women's Aid Society because of the needs presented by the fire. She designated certain rooms to serve as the distribution headquarters for clothing as donations came in from across the country.

"I was unexpectedly forced into work of various kinds. It crowded us from every side," wrote Emma.[21] Her abilities to organize and conduct schools helped her to react quickly to the overwhelming needs caused by the fire. She founded an employment agency, a women's aid office, a food/clothing and toy bank, and began an industrial education program at the YWCA. Emma was a busy woman. Pushing aside her personal worries, she plunged into work, doing everything she could to aid the poor and redeem the lost. The needs were constant and overwhelming.

The days sped by quickly, and, before she knew it, Christmas had arrived. Many Chicagoans were still impoverished, but the aid societies had done much to provide temporary housing and work for men and women. Emma felt satisfied now that her life was making a difference.

On New Year's Day, she found herself sitting around a table where Moody and other local church leaders were present. Moody, a short, stocky, bearded man, asked each person to choose a Bible verse that would serve as their inspiration for the year to come. Moody shared his verse of choice— Isaiah 50:7, "For the Lord God will help me; therefore shall I not be confounded; therefore I have set my face like a flint, and I know that I shall not be ashamed."

As Moody looked at the faces of the men and women at the table, servants of God who he deeply respected, he said, "The world has yet to see what God would do with a man fully devoted to His service. I hope to be that man." Emma nodded. She, too, wanted to serve God with all of her heart and the very best of her ability.[22]

In a private conversation following the meeting, Moody challenged Emma not to return to her career as a schoolteacher. "That is good work for its kind; but there are teachers enough, who want to teach school, and schools enough that want them," said Moody. "But there ain't enough to do THIS work, and this is the best work." Moody's language wasn't fancy, no doubt his grammar irritated the proper schoolteacher, but his point was sharp and accurately reflected the change that had been happening in

Emma's heart over the past few years. "I became deeply interested in what Mr. Moody called 'the best work'," said Emma.[23]

Later that evening, she prayed to God asking for His guidance in her life. She asked friends of hers, near and far, to pray with her, asking that she might understand God's will for her life. Each of them wrote back to her, saying "yes" she should remain in Christian work. Emma resigned from her teaching career and began to do what Moody had deemed the "best work" of Christian education in Chicago.

During the next few years, D. L. Moody would begin to talk with Emma about a dream that she held dear—to create a training school for young men and women who could be trained for Christian service in the church, in Sunday schools, and missions, and to serve families everywhere. She and Moody could not do this work alone, God needed to train many more dedicated workers—and she could help accomplish that goal. After all, she was an educator. Her love for the Bible and her trained ability to teach others could be used by God to raise up a great army of Christian workers.

She did not realize that this simple dream would grow into an organized and far reaching plan and a school that would serve the church for decades to come.

CHAPTER SIX

Building a Bible School

Emma pressed her pencil so hard upon the parchment that the lead snapped. With each word, her penmanship became increasingly slanted and bold. She underlined words to emphasize how deeply she cared and how extremely upset she was.

"How could Mr. Moody withdraw his support?" she thought. "How could we build such a wonderful work of God only to see it crumble and dissolve?"

She had to be bold. The moment called for it. She refused to back down. With this letter, she would confront Mr. Moody and demand that he pay attention to the work in Chicago. He could not go back on his promises to the school and to her. She set her jaw into a hard, determined line. She had not come this far only to be dismissed. It just wasn't in her nature.

It had been more than fifteen long and difficult years since Emma's original dream to build a Bible school for training Christian workers. After the Chicago fire, Emma followed Mr. Moody's call to leave behind her teaching. She went to work among the urban poor, convinced that the "impoverished masses" needed to know God's Word just as much as they needed food and shelter.

Because Emma had lost everything in the fire, she moved in with two women known as the Kirkland sisters.[24] Mr. Moody's church work continued to grow. At the same time, he was preparing to leave for an international tour of evangelistic meetings. Before he did so, he purchased land to build his church at Chicago Avenue and La Salle Street, the present location of Moody Bible Institute.

The devastated city of Chicago had lost more than residences; also gone were key establishments, like schools, churches, and charities. Under Emma's organized leadership, many of these organizations were reestablished, and Bible teaching became a focus. Her practical schools grew quickly to draw as many as three hundred children and four hundred women. As a part of the Chicago Bible work, she established a daily morning school for children who could not attend public school. The industrial schools, as they were called, taught both educational and trade skills to the children of immigrants. They also offered a sewing school for women on Saturdays.[25]

In addition, Emma's workers visited thousands of homes throughout Chicago, reading the Bible, praying, and visiting the sick. She was organized to a fault and kept each worker on task, admonishing them if they were not dressed appropriately. The women, attired in long, floor-length full skirts in dark, sensible material and high-collared white blouses, were required to report on how many doors they knocked and on how many Bible portions were distributed.[26]

Her work, though satisfying, was also tiring. Emma did not like to live alone and sometimes signed her letters "from Lonesome Boulevard." Although she was an accomplished and busy woman, the serious-minded Emma sometimes longed for companionship. Some say she harbored an unrequited love.[27]

Ever since she had moved out of her parents' home in New York, Emma had lived in boardinghouses of one sort or another, sometimes serving as the supervisor of the house. It was not unusual for unmarried women of the time to hold such positions. The houses typically had private bedrooms, but common meeting and dining areas. Simple meals were provided to boarders in the formal dining area three times a day. Individual rooms were lit by kerosene lamps and fresh water was provided each morning for washing. In Chicago, she often roomed with other Christian workers.

Emma also continued to struggle with her health. In addition to the physical weakness left behind after her bout with typhoid fever, she also suffered from an eye condition called diplopia or "double vision." The blurring made reading difficult, a tragedy for the Bible teacher, and brought on spells of dizziness. Emma devoted long hours of prayer to God asking for His healing from this eye condition. Once again, she experienced His merciful hand upon her life. She credited God for healing her from her vision problems.[28]

God also sent help in the form of friendship. One of her good friends and financial supporters, a Mrs. Cleveland, noticed that Emma was exhausted. She came for a visit and, after they had a cup of tea and caught up on the news of the Bible work in Chicago, Mrs. Cleveland pressed two pieces of paper into her hand.

Emma looked at it in surprise. In her hand she held a train ticket and one hundred dollars, a considerable sum to the frugal schoolteacher. "I've bought you a ticket to New York," said her friend. "You haven't rested once since the fire, and I'm going to send you home to your mother. The ticket is good for a year. Stop over as often as you want and stay as long as you want. All we want is that you come back."[29]

Emma's eyes filled with tears at the unexpected generosity of the gift. God had met her unspoken needs with this kind act of a wealthy friend. "It was sacred to me," wrote Emma. "I put it into the most consecrated place I know."[30]

We do not know if Emma ever used that ticket to visit her mom, but she would soon learn that both of her parents had died in 1876. That same year, she followed Mr. Moody to New York City where he was speaking to huge crowds at a leased space in the circus magnate P. T. Barnum's Hippodrome, now called Madison Square Garden. The New York venue had housed circus acts and boxing, but now featured the preaching of God's Word. The four-month-long revival drew as many as 11,000 people each night.[31]

While Emma was happy to see Mr. Moody, she had come to the city with business on her mind. She wanted to urge the evangelist to return to Chicago and to help her finally establish the Bible school they had dreamed of before the fire. But Moody, distracted by the important and very successful work being done in New York, was undecided and contemplating whether or not Chicago was ready for a full-fledged Bible school.

Emma, knowing she only had time for a few words, spoke pointedly. She said, "I hope, Mr. Moody, you will decide, for your indecision hinders other Christian work."[32]

Discouraged and frustrated, Emma returned to Chicago alone. Moody would not follow until the end of the year, and, even then, he would be continuing his travels, preaching at evangelistic meetings, with little to no attention being paid to their plans for a school.

By 1878, Emma's Chicago Bible work had grown and the beginning of a formal school was emerging. She supervised seventeen adult students who were enrolled in the training school that she had envisioned so many years before. The program was described as a "year of study and experimental services." The Bible workers could either live in their own homes or in the house provided by the Woman's Council under Dryer's supervision. The fledgling school attracted some international students as well who were eager to study the Scriptures in English.[33]

The students enrolled in formal classes including Bible study, Bible history, and methods of Christian work. She invited pastors, evangelists, and physicians to lecture the students. Emma's Bible workers made house to house visits among those they considered "destitute." While most of the people they visited lived in tenement housing and were financially poor, the workers viewed "destitute" as meaning a lack of religious faith and training. Emma and her workers viewed God's Word and education as the primary solution to social problems.[34]

One thing that Emma Dryer and D. L. Moody had in common was their dedication to their work, even at the expense of their personal well-being. By 1879, both the evangelist and Dryer were emotionally and physically depleted. Moody was on the verge of a collapse. He was back and forth to England and the States, then traveling between New York, New England, and Chicago.[35]

Dryer decided to take a brief leave from the Chicago work and left for Scotland in 1879. She traveled to England, attending Bible conferences, visiting, and observing work at the London Deaconess House and at the YMCA. The work in England, like hers in Chicago, was directed toward the urban poor, and she learned a great deal from her travels abroad.[36]

By 1883, Moody and Dryer were both back in Chicago with renewed hope to develop their school. Supporters of their cause met weekly to pray for God's leading and direction. Emma Dryer met with Charles Blanchard, the president of Wheaton College, who encouraged her to begin "trial sessions" of this type of Bible institute. Encouraged by Blanchard, she began fund-raising. Almost immediately, she received $500 in support of the proposed school.

Emma wanted quality teaching, so she set out to contact and recruit the very best faculty. For their first session, they had fifty male and female students meeting in the YMCA, and named the fledgling school the May Institute.[37]

In 1884, the second session of May Institute grew to seventy-five students. Finally, Moody took notice. In January of 1886, he returned to Chicago and addressed a large group of influential men at Farwell Hall. He challenged these supporters to raise $250,000. If they did so, he assured them, he would return to Chicago and found the Bible institute.[38]

Emma took the challenge to heart. In the spring of 1885, she began the work of fund-raising. One of her first significant contributions was $50,000 from her wealthy friend Nettie McCormick and Nettie's son, Cyrus. Another $100,000 came from Texas cattle rancher John Farwell. Things were looking up.[39]

Politically, in 1886, Chicago was in turmoil. The city population had grown to more than 500,000, doubling in size in just ten years. The Haymarket Riot had captured the attention of the city and violent rioting broke out between the labor class and the police. Four men were hanged in what historians now see as a rash act of justice. Emma was captivated by the proceedings and even attended the trial. She wrote, "We are a government blamable for letting anarchy grow on this soil. We ought to strangle it . . . we are not teaching in our schools the principles of sound government. The feeling of do-as-you-like is alarmingly fostered and we shan't stop anarchy by hanging even its justly contemned leaders. We must go deeper down."[40]

Emma saw the Bible and Bible training as the only proper solution to society's evils. It renewed her energy to press on toward the founding of the school. As Emma worked hard to find donors and raise the $250,000 challenged by Mr. Moody, the evangelist had returned to New York. After many meetings and long conversations, Emma finally secured the amount of money needed to begin.

Emma wrote of that time, "The Christian associations of those years were an unspeakable blessing. They awoke my constant gratitude unto God. My thanksgiving of them will be heard until the melodies of Heaven."[41] Emma felt that finally she could see the light at the end of a long tunnel. The school she had prayed for and worked toward could finally begin. All that was missing was Mr. Moody himself.

In her excitement to begin, Emma wrote to Moody demanding that he now return to Chicago and keep his promise. Moody did not react kindly to her letter, taking her forthright manner as confrontational and offensive.

He wrote back . . . not to congratulate her on raising the funds—but to tell her that he was quitting, leaving the work in Chicago, and bringing the school to New York.[42]

Emma was angry. She was so furious she could hardly contain her temper. Some had called her "mercurial" and her emotions flew as high as the red on a glass thermometer. How could Moody betray her, betray all of them, like this? How could Moody call her to leave her teaching career only to desert her at the last and most crucial moment?

Furious, she wrote a letter to the evangelist, her hand shaking as she underlined her words multiple times to emphasize the depth of her emotion. "Through loneliness and trouble, and constant, wearing work, I have held on. When others doubted, I believed. When others hurried away, I prayed on, and worked on. When others said you never meant to come here [to Chicago], I believed that God had made you [Moody] speak the truth . . . and I prayed on."[43]

Emma's words showed her desperation to get Moody's attention. She added to the letter: "I dare not—though this provocation be dangerously distressing—leave my post, let the enemy triumph. Do not you leave yours![44]

Emma's words, as rash and angry as they might appear, ultimately saved the school. At her heeding, along with the intervention of his wife and of the philanthropist Nettie McCormick, Moody reconsidered and agreed to meet with his donors in Chicago.

On February 5, 1887, Moody called a meeting with donors to found the Chicago Evangelization Society. This is the school that would ultimately be renamed in his honor: the Moody Bible Institute.

For those first classes, students enrolled in three-month terms. They studied Bible Exposition, Geography of Bible Lands, Christian Evidences, Church History, Methods of Evangelism, and Church Work. Students paid fifty dollars room and board for a three-month term, but, in a tradition that continues to this day, tuition was free to those who came.[45]

Even though the Chicago Evangelization Society was now established, Emma Dryer continued to struggle with both Moody and the board. She wanted to retain her sense of control. Ironically, even though her wish had come true and she now had Mr. Moody's full attention, she now no longer had her independence. Some say Emma herself was the problem at the young school. She was outspoken and said exactly what was on her mind. She was sometimes openly critical of people who did not meet her precise standards and would speak so plainly that she often wounded those around her.

In 1889, the Chicago Bible Society incorporated and Emma withdrew from her full-time work with Moody to focus more on the Bible work with the CBS. She continued to do what she loved the most, supervise the women making home visits around the city.

Women continued to visit the homes of the poorest families of Chicago. The women wore beautiful dresses of "dark navy blue serge" and bonnets of the same color. In photos, they appear very serious and the homes that they visit are heartbreakingly impoverished. The children, standing in the street, wear tattered clothing and bare feet.[46]

Although Emma's formal association with Moody had ended, their relationship remained cordial and respectful. In 1903, she retired officially from the Chicago Evangelization Society and was named Superintendent Emeritus. Emma lived in a woman's home in Chicago and was committed to urban and foreign missions for the remainder of her life.[47]

On April 16, 1925, at the age of ninety, Emma Dryer had a slight stroke and lingered until dying at 11 p.m. Funeral services were held in her home. Harold McCormick, a descendant of the family who had so generously supported the early Bible work, paid for the entire funeral and sent an "automobile load of beautiful flowers."[48] Emma Dryer was finally at rest, gone to meet the God she had so faithfully served.

Emma was remembered for her considerable intellectual ability. The Chicago Bible Society said they desired to put on record their deep appreciation of her Christian work and their personal, affectionate regard for her: "Most gratifying of all has been our unquestioned confidence in the Christian consecration of Superintendent and Workers as we have seen their constant daily duties 'done heartily as unto the Lord.'"[49]

A friend of the family wrote, "She was a lovely and gracious woman with a keen intellect and unusual gifts and ability, all consecrated to the service of Him, her Lord and Savior."[50] D. L. Moody called Emma Dryer "the best teacher of the Word of God in the United States."[51]

CHAPTER SEVEN

Women and Education

While we may take education for granted, women at the turn of the century were not guaranteed that opportunity.

For African-American children in the 1800s, even a basic, childhood education, like learning to read, write, and calculate sums, was a rare opportunity. As late as 1830, North Carolina had a state law that "forbade all persons to teach slaves to read or write."[1] Both Mary McLeod Bethune and Amanda Berry Smith, daughters of slaves, tell of their limited opportunities to attend classes as young girls. Their education was spotty at best, even when they were welcomed into classrooms started by missionaries.

Even when black children *were* allowed into the classroom, it was difficult for them to attend regularly. They usually had to walk a great distance to these fledgling schools and were needed at home to help with work in the fields. These hardships made education almost totally dependent on the efforts of parents, and most grew up without access to books.

For white children, education was becoming the norm, but when Emma Dryer and Nettie McCormick attended school beyond their teen years, they were making an unusual choice. At the time, the majority only attended school during their childhood. For Fanny Crosby, education for the blind was a novel concept, yet it was something Fanny yearned for—she wanted to be treated like other children—she wanted to learn.

In 1848, a Women's Rights Convention was held in Seneca Falls, New York. One of the main concerns of the women gathered there was that women were being denied access to higher education. In her article "Early College Women: Determined to Be Educated," Maggie Lowe explains, "Women did not have access to higher education before 1848. While a few women might attend a female seminary or academy, they were not allowed into colleges or universities."[2]

The Civil War changed the expectations for females. As women were faced with cares and responsibilities beyond the home, they began to demand more rights to education. They wanted to attend the same colleges that men attended, not merely the "sister colleges." They wanted to study subjects that did not necessarily focus on the home like math and science, history and theology.

At that time, many schools focused on preparing women to be better wives and mothers. Two types of advanced education institutions were popular: "academies" and "seminaries." Academies did not require women to attend for any set period of time, and many of the curriculums were similar to a finishing school. The schools focused on teaching girls practical things like how to cook, sew, supervise servants, and track household expenses.

One school advertised, "St. Mary's is a school for young women who desire to continue their work two or three years beyond the course of the high school. It is a school where girls become better daughters; where they are systematically trained for the duties of wifehood and motherhood; where they are encouraged to recognize, and where they are required to prepare for, their present and future obligations."[3] Many people were concerned that higher education would make women "unfit" for marriage and motherhood.[4] In a sense they were right, since as many as 50 percent of women who attended college delayed marriage or did not marry at all.

The Female Seminary Movement began around 1815, and encouraged a more serious purpose than the academies. As the demand for education increased, many other types of "colleges" and "seminaries" developed, some with the main purpose of training women as teachers. They were called "normal schools." Emma Dryer attended one such school in Illinois, which is now known as Illinois State University. While normal schools offered their primary coursework in teacher training, they still devoted a good portion of their curriculum to "domestic science" and "home economics."

However, despite the opening of many new colleges, female numbers remained low. By 1890, only 0.7 percent of women attended college. In 1900, it climbed to an impressive 2.8 percent.[5] Despite their low numbers, these early female college graduates began to influence society. They were among the first to become involved in politics and then demanded the right to vote. They expressed opinions about women's rights and insisted on regulations that would protect children, both in factories and in the home.

When Emma Dryer began a school in Chicago, the May Institute, her particular interest was Bible and ministry education for women. As a Christian, she believed that Bible knowledge was the key to bettering both the home and society, and that women could and should be effectively trained in the Bible. Many of the early class photos of the Chicago school show many women, who came from every part of the United States to study the Bible and devote their life to Christian service.

Education was changing in the United States—and women were a key part of that change.

"NETTIE" NANCY (FOWLER) MCCORMICK

1835–1923

CHAPTER EIGHT

Love and Marriage

Nettie studied her reflection in the bedroom mirror. Her brown hair was neatly pulled back and pinned up, parted in the center. Her fashionable Paris gown, especially ordered for the occasion, touched the floor—its soft dove-grey color appropriate for the occasion. The long sleeves would help stave off the Chicago winter chill that crept in through the walls.

For today's wedding ceremony, she would carry a small Bible into a room adorned with garlands of flowers and white tapers in silver candelabras. A marriage was always a great cause for celebration and many details had gone into the preparations for this special day. Any minute now, her uncle would knock at the door and escort her down to the parlor where some five hundred guests were waiting for the marriage ceremony to begin and the elaborate dinner party to follow.

Today, January 28, 1858, was the day she would marry the handsome, wealthy inventor of the reaper, Cyrus McCormick. Some people had whispered disapproval of the marriage between two so widely separated by age. She wasn't surprised by their questions. Cyrus was twenty-five years her senior. But, Nettie felt, they were alike in the most important ways of all— and she would not let popular opinion dissuade her. At age twenty-two, she was certainly not a young bride, and some may have wondered if she would end up an old maid. But then she had met Cyrus, and her world had forever been changed.

Cyrus was tall and distinguished with a full dark beard. He had kind eyes and a forthright, serious disposition. Most importantly, he loved her. Cyrus had told her, when he proposed:

"I do not think there is a man in the world who would strive more to please you than I should do—no one whose disposition and manner would be more under your control and influence than mine as your husband."[1]

His words thrilled Nettie's heart, and she was convinced that they were a good match. She and Cyrus agreed on the value of family and commitment to God's work in the community. She admired his energy and drive. He was a serious and wealthy man, but he was also kind and true.

Her only regret was that on this most important day of her life, her wedding day, her parents would not be present. Nettie, as she was now called, was born Nancy Fowler on February 8, 1835. Her father, Melza Fowler, had been a merchant in Brownsville, New York. However, Nancy never knew him. When she was just seven months old, he died in a tragic accident.

On a business trip, her father's horses were causing problems for the stable workers at the hotel where he was staying. The workers were unable to enter the stall to feed the tired and hungry animals. When her father finally came down to the stables and attempted to enter the stall, his own horse reared and struck him with a blow to the head. He died three days later.[2]

Nettie's mother, Clarissa, took over the household, caring for her and her brother. They lived in a small town and would often ride to school on their horse, Nettie seated up front and holding on to its mane. But when Nettie was just seven years old, tragedy struck the family again and their mother died. Now orphans, Nettie and her brother moved to Clayton, New York, to live with their grandmother and uncle in their well-to-do home on the St. Lawrence River.[3]

People said Nettie was a serious child. Certainly, the loss of both of her parents at such a young age had contributed to her solemn and introspective personality. But her grandmother and her uncle also influenced young

Nettie in positive ways. Uncle Eldridge had a solid faith and strong work ethic and was active in both his community and church. He also believed that young women, just like young men, should get an education.

Uncle Eldridge made sure Nettie was able to attend school as long as she would like. She attended Falley Seminary in Fulton, Emma Willard's newly founded Troy Female Seminary, and the Genesee Wesleyan Seminary in Lima, New York. She studied geography, history, theology, French, and music. She loved music more than the rest and considered geography "one of the hardest textbooks in school."[4]

Nettie was a good student, but sometimes found it trying. "I am prospering in my studies," she wrote in her journal. "Am trying to still live a Christian amid all the temptations of a boarding school. I make many crooked paths, but my strength is my savior."[5]

During her teen years, Nettie became active in a missionary society and was asked to teach for two years in the little school she had attended in Clayton. Despite her hardships at a young age, her life had seemed to progress steadily along. That is, until she met the man who had changed her life: Cyrus McCormick.

Cyrus McCormick was an inventor who had made a fortune with his reaping machine. Growing up on a farm in Virginia, he had watched his father and others toil in the fields. When Nettie was just one year old, Cyrus had patented the machine and began to produce them on the farm. In 1847, he moved to Chicago to establish a factory and successful business ventures and became one of the most well-known industrialists in America's history.

In the fall of 1856, Nettie had come to visit her cousin Maria in Chicago. She stayed through the winter with the family. One chilly day, as she was walking on a bridge over the Chicago River, she was passed by the carriage of the McCormick brothers. Cyrus McCormick, who was returning from the factory with his brother Leander spotted Nettie walking down the street. "Who is that beautiful woman?" he asked. His brother did not know, but said he would ask his wife. Quickly an afternoon tea was arranged at the Leander McCormick home and Nettie was invited, so the two could meet.[6]

Cyrus was a fast and determined worker. He went right over to speak with Nettie. Leading her to a sofa, he introduced himself and inquired about her situation. Nettie was flattered that such a handsome and indus-trious man would be interested in her. The next day, at noon, Cyrus stopped by her cousin's home to hear Nettie sing, and returned each day afterward to take her for rides in his carriage.

When Nettie returned East, he con-tinued to write her each day. He could not forget about the young woman with the deep brown eyes and beauti-ful voice. His cousin said that he spoke of his love for Nettie "a few days af-ter he met her." He proposed by mail, and, restless for her reply, went East to claim his bride.[7]

It was a courtship of determination and love that led the young couple to this important day: their wedding. In many ways, they had been extraordinarily blessed—with talent, wealth, ingenuity, and education. Even as a young child, Nettie had loved Christ's parable of the talents. She believed, and knew from her own childhood ex-perience, that life was too short not to make it count for something. She wrote in her diary, "How my bark [boat] hurries down the dark stream of times."[8]

Cyrus and Nettie never believed that their own personal happiness was the primary goal of life. They wanted to honor God and serve others. What would they do with the abundance that God had given them?

Cyrus and Nettie never believed that their own personal happiness was the primary goal of life. They wanted to honor God and serve others. What would they do with the abundance that God had given them?

CHAPTER NINE

Tremendous Riches and Devastating Loss

N ettie's face went white, the thin slip of paper trembling in her hand. She reread the terse message sent from their household staff in Chicago:

"City burned. Return on first train. Factory gone."

Burned? Gone? The couple was at their residence in New York when they received the horrifying news. As Cyrus made arrangements for a carriage, Nettie quickly began putting clothing into trunks, forgoing the usual careful lists that she would always make to organize their journeys.

She asked Cyrus to go send a telegraph, but the man said he couldn't send a message to Chicago because there wasn't any Chicago: Chicago was burned.

It was October 1871, and the Chicago fire had roared through the city, leaving thousands homeless and practically nothing standing in its wake. The city was burning, and with it the McCormick home and factory. The McCormicks took the next train to Chicago. The train went until it could go no farther, the tracks disappearing at the edge of the charred, ruined city.

They were met by a carriage just south of the city. Nettie could not believe her eyes. Together they went to view the smoking ruins of what had been their factory. Then, even more slowly, the driver turned the horses toward the remnants of their home. It had been thirteen years since they had married on that wintry January day in Chicago. Thirteen years filled with great successes, but also tremendous loss. The fire that destroyed their home was just another hurdle they would have to face together.

In the first two years following their Chicago wedding, the McCormicks lived in Washington, D.C. Cyrus was involved in legal battles over rival inventors for his patent on the reaper. Despite these challenges, the company grew and expanded internationally. The McCormicks became increasingly wealthy and important members of Chicago's elite. They enjoyed traveling to Europe, and Nettie, not quite the typical nineteenth century wife, was determined to learn the business. From the start, she was active in important business decisions. She was noted for her unusual and precise memory. She could recall the smallest details and was able to keep track of many activities at once with the utmost precision.[9]

The McCormicks were extremely wealthy, but also abundantly generous. They gave to causes they believed in—particularly religious education and missions. One year after they were married, Cyrus gave a gift of $100,000 to a Presbyterian seminary and had it moved to Chicago—where he believed they could educate even more people in God's Word.[10] The seminary was renamed the McCormick Theological Seminary. Nettie loved the idea that they were investing their temporary riches in the eternal value of God's Word.

It was also during those early years that Nettie discovered she would often be alone. Cyrus had heavy demands on his personal time and was often called from home for business. In many ways, his life was not his own—and the obligations of his wealth were many. As a new bride, and soon a new mother, Nettie struggled with loneliness. She also was adjusting to her role as a woman of importance in society. Everything she did and said was noticed and critiqued by others. "It sounds very easy, but it is not easy to be really good," wrote Nettie, "and always put forth the best effort, to study wise words, to say the right thing in the right place. This is not easy."[11]

The couple was overjoyed to begin a family. Nettie had always wanted to be a mother, and soon she and Cyrus were blessed with the arrival of children: Cyrus Hall Jr. and Mary Virginia. But despite these early blessings, they were not always joyous. In 1865, their third child, Robert, died. Nettie then suffered several miscarriages and her fifth child, Alice, also died as an infant. She was devastated by the loss of these precious lives.

Nettie wondered if the death of her children was a sign of God's punishment for laziness or procrastination—sins that she struggled to overcome. Why would the God she served allow her to lose these dear babies?[12] Although the McCormicks were blessed with three more children—Anita, Harold, and Stanley—her struggles as a mother continued to an even greater degree later in life. Two of her children, Mary Virginia and Stanley, developed severe mental illness, requiring them to be under private medical care and isolated from society. During those moments, Nettie struggled to see God's hand.

In addition to the troubles with her children, at age thirty-four Nettie began to lose her hearing. Doctors were unable to diagnose the condition that left the woman almost completely deaf. She would carry a small trumpet that, when held to the ear, could amplify sound and allow her to carry on conversations. The deafness would continue for the next fifteen years.[13]

Friends do not remember Nettie being discouraged by her personal disability. She refused to allow her deafness to limit her ability to communicate with others. One friend remembers, "She always had something of tremendous importance to say, either to the table at large or to the one particular person who interested her that day."[14]

Despite her personal troubles, Nettie continued to trust in God. One friend remarked, "She had the most marvelous spiritual life. She had a personal God whom she wrestled with in prayer and supplication and whom she served all day long. I think that she lived by that inspiration a great deal."[15]

Nettie resolved that she could never fully understand the ways of God. She wrote, "We plan—and God steps in with another plan for us, and He is all wise and the most loving friend we have always helping us."[16]

Perhaps it was not as surprising then, when the Chicago fire occurred, in 1871. It came at a time of transition in their lives. Cyrus was nearing retirement and wondered if the fire was a sign he should officially quit the business. Nettie disagreed. "Rebuild," she said. "I do not wish our sons to grow up in idleness."[17] She felt the McCormick Harvesting Machine Company should continue—both for the good of the workers who depended on the factory for income and for their children. She did not want her sons to grow up as wealthy heirs with little or no responsibility.

Following the fire, the McCormick family built a grand estate at 675 North Rush Street in Chicago. The home boasted a formal entryway with painted ceilings, enormous urns, oriental carpets, and mahogany furniture. Portraits of the McCormick family adorned the walls. A large garden occupied an entire plot of land next to the building. The mansion was so dominant in the neighborhood that many called the area "McCormickville."[18]

While the McCormicks had the financial means needed to rebuild their home and factory, most other citizens were devastated by the fire. The city depended on the generosity and determination of the wealthy and local charities to house the homeless and feed the hungry. Nettie was honored to use her abundant resources to support these worthy causes.

Women like mission worker Sarah Dunn Clarke were the recipients of Nettie's charitable giving. Nettie wrote a personal note to Sarah, saying: "I often think of you, and the noble work you have done for humanity in the Pacific Garden Mission. I should love to see you, if even only for a few minutes."[19]

Those years also saw the growth of an unusual friendship between Cyrus and a young evangelist named Dwight L. Moody, a man eighteen years his junior. Cyrus had heard Moody preach and admired the man's spirit. The two men got along extremely well, perhaps bonded by their similar personalities, full of energy and determination. Nettie became close friends with one of Moody's coworkers, Emma Dryer. She and Emma spent many hours in conversation discussing Emma's outreach work with women and the poor of Chicago and Moody's plan to begin a Chicago school for Christian workers.

In response to Emma's request, Cyrus gave a sizeable donation to Moody to begin establishing his school. During those years, Moody was a frequent visitor in the McCormick home for meals. The entire family would attend his meetings. At one revival, Moody preached to ten thousand with courage and conviction. In the audience stood his friends Cyrus and Nettie, joining in the singing.

While he was able to see the fruit of his donations to McCormick Theological Seminary, Cyrus would not live to see Mr. Moody's school become a reality. In 1880, he suffered a stroke that left him paralyzed. Four years later, in 1884, Cyrus McCormick died, leaving Nettie a wealthy widow. Following his death, his son Cyrus Jr. was named president of the company, while Nettie retained her role as financial advisor.

Cyrus McCormick died a wealthy and world-renowned man, but also a man of deep and unwavering commitment to God. According to one biographer, his last words were simply, "It's all right. It's all right. I only want heaven."[20]

While Cyrus entered his heavenly home, Nettie would face many more years without him on this earth. She had a business to run, a family to attend, and a great deal of money to give away.

CHAPTER TEN

The Wealthiest Woman in Chicago

Y es, money is power," said Nettie. "But I have always tried not to trust in it, but rather use it for the glory of my Master."[21]

The headline in the June 1917 Chicago Daily News read: "Mrs. McCormick Leads Women on Tax Lists." The article went on to say, "Mrs. N. F. McCormick, widow of the senior Cyrus McCormick, inventor of the McCormick Reaper, pays the largest personal property tax of any woman in Chicago, according to the 1917 records of the county assessors who valued her at $895,000."[22]

Nettie stayed busy after Cyrus's death, but she missed him terribly. Cyrus Jr., when he took over the factory for his father, was only in his twenties, so Nettie remained heavily involved in the details and business decisions of the operation. She was busy, yes, but also grieving the loss of her partner.

Geraldine Beeks, a factory supervisor who came to see Nettie about some business matters, noticed Mrs. McCormick's distress when they passed by a portrait of her late husband. Gazing for a moment at his portrait, Nettie turned to the woman and said softly, "It's very lonely, Miss Beeks. It's very lonely."[23]

Perhaps to alleviate her sadness, Nettie immersed herself in both the factory and her charitable work. Unfortunately, just two years after Cyrus died, in 1886, a distressing event occurred. For several years, there had been growing tensions between laborers and factory owners. In the spring of 1886, the workers at the McCormick Harvesting Machine Company went on strike demanding a shorter work week. A protest outside of the plant resulted in one person being killed.

That event triggered a larger protest at the Haymarket Square in Chicago. The meeting, which had begun in a peaceful manner, erupted into violence. A bomb was thrown and police fired on the crowd. Seven policemen and four civilians were killed. Hundreds were injured. The bombing was blamed on a group of anarchists and people demanded their execution.

The trial became a huge spectacle—and Nettie was dismayed. The McCormick name was frequently associated with the trial that ended with seven men being sentenced to death. Emma Dryer, Nettie's friend, attended the trial and wrote to comfort her friend and shed God's perspective on the events. "There is no justice possible outside of Christ. Law centers in Him, and as I hear these arguments from a social standpoint, my heart aches to have the church of Christ see where her work lies."

Emma knew that her dear friend, who had been such a great help to her and Mr. Moody in starting a school, was still grieving the loss of her husband. She wrote, "Dear Mrs. McCormick, when you are prone in your grief—I have been there. When you are numb with mental pain—I have been there; when you are exhausted with thinking and wondering, I have been there; when you know only one thing—that Jesus of Nazareth lived and died according to the gospels, I have been there! In my deeper thoughts and feelings, you have so continuous a share."[24]

Emma Dryer and Nettie McCormick were unusual friends. One single, the other married. One lived on a frugal income; the other was enormously wealthy. One was known for being rigid and a bit prudish, while the other for being lenient and compassionate. Yet, despite their differences, the two women cared deeply for each other and were deeply invested in causes that they each believed in.

It was Nettie who came to Emma's defense when D. L. Moody wanted to set aside the Chicago work for other pursuits. She wrote a forcible letter to Mr. Moody on Emma's behalf offering her opinion. Without the intervention of both women, along with Moody's wife, Moody Bible Institute would not have become a reality.

At one point, the Chicago school was facing a deficit of four thousand dollars which had to be promptly paid. Moody, who believed in the power of prayer, asked God to send the needed money. While he was on the platform at a large meeting, a messenger brought in an urgent letter. He said it came from Mrs. McCormick. Moody's assistant, thinking it was an invitation to lunch, opened it and found, instead, a check for three thousand dollars. Afterward, Nettie told Moody that she had felt a strong urging to send money. She couldn't get rid of the thought from her mind, and knew that it must be sent that very day. When she learned that the actual amount needed exceeded her gift, she sent another check.[25]

She admired Moody's work and continued to support the work of the Institute through gifts. When Moody set up a tent to preach at the World's Fair—taking the controversial approach of sharing a space with a circus act—Nettie wrote a letter of approval saying she appreciated his "unique way of moving the masses."[26]

Nettie's charitable giving extended beyond Chicago, to schools and organizations across the United States and even abroad. Friends said that Nettie had been "animated by one great purpose—the spread of Christianity, Christian education, and western medicine all over the world."[27] She never wanted personal acclaim for these gifts.

Those at McCormick Theological Seminary noticed that when three of the buildings she funded were dedicated, Nettie was always out of town.

"Each time there was a good reason for her absence, but no one who knew her doubted that she was more content to avoid such publicity."[28]

She was very selective in which institutions she supported and also liked to make sure the money was used properly. "Those who knew her ways closely have said, with pardonable exaggeration, that she knew every stick and brick in any building that she gave."[29] One day, when trees were being planted in front of one of the new buildings she had funded, Nettie was concerned they were not being placed correctly.

She asked her coachman to drop her in front of the building, and exited the coach carrying a pair of "immensely tall rubber boots." Once in the parlor, Nettie sat and put on the boots, then announced she was going outside to superintend the planting of the trees. All morning, she stood in the snow, "slender and graceful," in those huge boots, until she had made certain that every tree was planted safely in the proper spot.[30] That was just Nettie's way.

Some of her giving was instigated by her travels. On a trip to Egypt, she visited two missionary schools and made generous gifts to support the building of dormitories. She was heartbroken by the plight of women in that country: "They do not read, they are not thought worthy to kneel in mosques," wrote Nettie.[31]

She was heavily involved with several schools in the South. She became interested in the welfare of the southern Appalachians, which led her to help finance the Home Industrial School in Asheville, North Carolina. In South Carolina, she established the Thornwell Orphanage.

Overseas, she funded buildings at the Shantung Christian University, the University of Nanking, and the North China Union University in China. She also helped establish Bible schools in Korea. One woman remembered, "Ever since I was a little girl, I had been told about her. All my teachers came from her schools. She is a living monument to all of the Korean people. She has done so much for Korea—giving schools a spirit of international love from people so far away."[32]

Although the McCormicks did have lavish homes, including a new home built in Lake Forest in her later years, Nettie always put charity ahead of personal desires. Once, near Christmas time, she looked around their home and said, "We need new curtains, but I think I would rather spend it for a school."[33]

Throughout her years as a widow, Nettie remained involved in the McCormick business and with her family. She was an attentive and giving friend, and a generous benefactor. It was no wonder then, that when her eightieth birthday approached, her daughter Anita and others began to plan a celebration.

They knew that Nettie would not want a big fuss and certainly no accolades, so they had to be secretive.

It was a beautiful sunny and mild day in February. Everything was arranged in advance and it was decided that it should be at Nettie's home; the party must come to her. In the morning, Anita came and took her mom for a ride, while the staff readied the home. When they returned home, she told her mother that a few friends might be joining them for tea, and suggested she put on her new dress, a gray silk satin with silver brocade trim.[34]

As they went downstairs, people started to arrive, a small number at first, and then lines to greet Nettie and to thank her for what she had meant in their lives. A group of employees who had been at McCormick Works for many years, working men, arrived carrying eighty roses.

The *Herald*, on February 9, 1915, reported that "Mrs. McCormick at 80 Gets a World Tribute." The reporter wrote, "Letters, telegrams, cablegrams, and congratulations by personal messenger came to Mrs. McCormick from nearly every state in the Union and from nearly every country in the world."[35]

"Leaders in Africa, in Syria, in Persia, in Siam, in many parts of China, in Japan, and in the Philippine Islands joined in. The simple surprise party ended as a festival such as ordinarily is arranged only for kings and queens."[36]

"To them, in a way," the reporter summarized, "she has given her life away."[37]

Nettie died in their Lake Forest home on July 5, 1923, at the age of eighty-eight. Her obituary said that Nettie McCormick had donated to six institutions, but later records revealed she had supported as many as 446 religious and educational institutions.[38] Her estate was valued at $15 million, which would amount to approximately $204 million today.

Yet she was remembered not so much for her material possessions, but for her warmth, gracious spirit, and generous personality. She cared about each person and took a vivid interest in the work of Christ, knowing that her treasure, truly, was in heaven.

SARAH DUNN CLARKE

1835–1918

CHAPTER ELEVEN

A Life of Privilege

S arah sat alone in the parlor of her family's Waterloo, Iowa, home. The room was beautifully decorated with ornate, flocked wallpaper and dark, carved mahogany furniture. Her mother had recently ordered draperies, and Sarah was helping to paint matching decorations on the window shades.

She squinted her eyes to study the intricate design. As she raised her brush to add a final detail, she was startled by a voice speaking to her, almost as if someone was in the room.

It said, "What are you doing to decorate your heavenly home?"

The question penetrated Sarah's twenty-six-year-old soul. She was not a shallow person by any means, but she had grown up in a family of wealth and privilege. In addition to making and receiving social calls, caring for the home was the primary obligation for most women of her day, and she had been quite content with this.

Sarah was born on November 13, 1835, in Cayuga County, New York. She was a slender young woman, only standing four feet ten inches tall and weighing no more than eighty-five pounds.[1] From a young age, she was raised in church and Sunday school. The Dunn family was appropriate and generally well-to-do. She was taught to stay away from worldly activities like playing cards, attending theatre, or participating in dances. But, she would later admit, she was also not particularly religious. She knew that she had never experienced a personal relationship with God.

As Sarah looked around her family's beautiful Victorian home, she started to consider the real purpose of her life. Should "God's precious and priceless time" be spent creating earthly decorations that would ultimately be destroyed? Why wasn't she spending time on things that really mattered? She realized that only souls "won for the Master would adorn the Heavenly mansion through all the cycles of eternity."[2]

After that day in the parlor where she heard God's prompting voice, reaching souls for Christ became the "passion of her life."[3] A few years later, Sarah moved to the growing urban center of Chicago. It was the 1860s, and the city was the furthest thing from the rural farmlands of Iowa.

The first railway to Chicago had been built just a few years earlier, in 1858, bringing people and commerce to the city. The beauty of Lake Michigan was contrasted by the clusters of buildings being built on the swampy land. In addition to meat packing and trade, Chicago's retail business district was developing. Potter Palmer, called the "Merchant Prince of Chicago," had bought almost a mile of what is now State Street. He widened the streets, built a hotel, and persuaded Marshall Field to open a store. Fashionable homes were being built on the south side of the city, and modern

Why wasn't she spending time on things that really mattered? She realized that only souls "won for the Master would adorn the Heavenly mansion through all the cycles of eternity."

conveniences like sewers and plumbing were being installed in residential homes.[4]

It was to this city that young Sarah arrived, most likely living with friends in a fashionable part of town. But even as she continued to live a sociable life, she eased her conscience by offering to help the city's destitute. More than 200,000 of the city's residents were jammed into small pine cottages in neighborhoods with no sewers or paved streets. Men, women, and children worked long hours for rock-bottom wages, struggling to put food on the table. The city was small and compact enough that the fashionable and the poor often crossed paths.[5]

Visiting the poor made her life feel shallow by comparison. She only felt God's approval and a "real soul satisfaction" when she was reaching out to those in need. As her list of needy families continued to grow, she joined several others to start a mission Sunday school on the corner of State and 23rd Streets.

It was also during these years that she met her husband, Colonel George Clarke. Born in New York in 1827, Clarke had been the editor of a newspaper and studied law before pursuing real estate. It was during those years that God had convicted him of his sin and given him, like Sarah, a higher calling in life.

In 1860, the Civil War broke out and Clarke returned to Chicago and joined other recruits in the 113th Illinois Volunteers. He was promoted to Major and then Lieutenant Colonel—before returning to Chicago to resume his real estate business in the now booming metropolis. During one of those business transactions, he became acquainted with a woman who would change the course of his life: Sarah Dunn.[6] Sarah found him to be devoted to good causes, but for more selfish reasons. She said that "he had always intended to be associated in some prominent enterprise in the Lord's cause, where his name could be engraven on marble or granite."[7] Clarke did not know that the Lord had other plans for his life.

The two found they had a great deal in common. Both moved in the same social circles, but they also had a desire to make their lives count. Certainly, they were challenged to reconsider life's purpose by the Chicago fire in 1871—an event that devastated the city. When the fire began, the town's wealthier residents attempted to pack up their most valued possessions. Some were seen burying their books, pianos, and china in the gardens behind their homes. They hired carriages and fled with whatever they could carry.[8]

Their efforts to protect their riches were almost ridiculously ineffective. The inferno of flames that charred nearly $200 million of property and left more than 100,000 homeless, completely eliminated homes, businesses, even the grandeur of Palmer's hotel and Field's department store. When the wealthy returned to the charred rubble that had been their homes, they found that even what was buried in their gardens had been completely destroyed.[9]

George and Sarah began to consider the value of things that were not perishable. The Chicago fire had quickly destroyed homes—those of the rich as well as the poor. Fortunes came and went. The cityscape had changed quickly—and churches were moving away from the worst parts of town infested by saloons, gambling halls, and brothels.

Just two years after the Chicago fire, in 1873, George asked Sarah to be his wife. They married on January 23, 1873, and settled in the Morgan Park neighborhood—a well-to-do section on the south of Chicago. But even though the two continued to move in fashionable circles, they could not help but think about "the deeper things of life." Clarke wondered whether he should continue to spend money on luxuries like Cuban cigars to entertain his wealthy friends, when he was doing so little to build up riches for the Lord.

Sarah persuaded her husband to join her in visiting the slums along the levee on South Clark Street, an area overflowing with drunkards and the outcasts of their society, male and female. Many of the stores in that area were rented for "barrel-houses" and saloons.[10] In addition to her house visits, twice a week, Sarah would spend afternoons visiting prisoners in the county jail.

After four years of marriage, they could no longer ignore God's prompting to do more. The couple opened a small rescue mission to reach the poor and to tell the gospel of Christ. On September 15, 1877, they rented a storefront at 386 South Clark Street, in the very heart of what people called "the devil's territory."

CHAPTER TWELVE

To Win One Soul

T he Clarkes' rescue mission was small and simply furnished. A few rows of plain wooden benches would seat about forty people. In the front sat a "wheezy" organ. Sarah painted Bible verses on large banners to decorate the brick walls. Flickering oil lamps lit the room and a potbellied stove tried to fight off the chilly Chicago weather.

The neighborhood was rough. The storefront they had rented was near a saloon, owned by "Hinky Dink" Kenna, a politically connected business owner in Chicago's vice district. Brothels and saloons lined the streets. In the first eight months following the Chicago fire, the city had granted more than two thousand saloon licenses—one saloon for every 150 residents. Crime and illegal activities took place shamelessly on the streets. Junkies would shoot up in public. Prostitutes would call out to passersby from doorways. It was into this district that the young couple fearlessly set up their mission.[11]

The first mission was surrounded on either side by saloons—and they could hear the banjos and instruments through the walls. George and Sarah were both involved in the mission services. While her husband would preach, Sarah said, "I tried to keep crooked men straight."

Some have said that George was the poorest preacher who ever tried to expound God's Word. He was not particularly eloquent, but he was deeply convicted and spoke emotionally about the condition of the lost. Tears would flow down his face freely as he talked to "boisterous audiences" at the mission.[12]

The men and women who attended those first meetings were often in "different degrees of intoxication," but that did not intimidate Sarah. With her husband, they would share the story of Jesus and His power to save. Often their talks would be interrupted by confusion and babbling brought on by too much liquor.[13]

It was not long before there were more people attending mission services than the small storefront would allow. So in 1880, George located larger quarters, at what is now 67 East Van Buren Street, in a building vacated by a notorious saloon called the Pacific Beer Garden. It was known as the "most murderous joint west of New York City."[14] It was located just down the street from the brothel district . . . just the place to establish their mission!

It was evangelist Dwight L. Moody, back from his evangelistic tours in England and establishing a Bible work in Chicago, who suggested the name. He said, "Why not just drop the 'Beer' and add the 'Mission'?" And so their small ministry gained its name: the Pacific Garden Mission.[15] Many students from Moody's school would help at the mission, singing and preaching.

The Clarkes found that running a mission was depleting their savings. Col. Clarke was no longer working in real estate, and the couple was devoting all of their time to the mission. Finances were at an all-time low, yet Sarah said, "We had a rich Father and we trusted Him."[16]

As they struggled to make ends meet, they began to look at the fine decorations and clothing in their Morgan Park home. It weighed upon their heart that their "indulgences" of former years could be sold and the money used to support their work. Sarah said, "We placed ALL upon the altar—all of our jewelry of every description. Diamonds, and other valued presents (with associations, too sacred to mention)—all alike was given to the Lord, for His cause—and for souls."[17]

They ran the mission with precision. Each night before the services, "Mother" Clarke as they called her would enter Room Twelve for prayer. Then she would take her place on the platform where George would read from the Bible. Together they worked to bring many souls to Christ. "They were an incomparable team of consecrated workers for God."[18]

One day, they found that they did not have enough money to pay the rent. They were unable to delay payment, so George and Sarah stayed up the entire night praying to God to send them the rent money. The work of the mission was going so well and demand for care was so pressing, that the Clarkes could not imagine shutting their doors, even for one night. They prayed for help and asked God to allow them to continue to trust in Him.

The next day, a miracle happened. When the Clarkes awoke, they found that the entire front yard of their home was covered with mushrooms. These were not ordinary mushrooms, but the best quality type and far ahead of season. They gathered the produce and sold it to the Palmer House Hotel. The payment was more than enough to pay the needed rent, with some left to spare. Sarah wrote of the event, "No mushrooms were ever seen there before—nor any since."[19]

In 1886, a group from the Pacific Garden Mission was singing near the corner of Van Buren and State Streets. People walking by would stop and listen for a moment. Three baseball players from the Chicago White Stockings ambled by that corner. They had been drinking at the saloons. Stumbling a bit, they sat down on the street corner to listen to the mission workers sing.

One of the players, named Billy, thought the songs reminded him of his mom, back in Iowa, and the Sunday school he had attended as a child. Silent tears rolled down his face, and he quickly bowed his head and brushed them aside. When the song ended, Sarah stood and addressed the small crowd, "Where is my wandering boy tonight?" she asked.

The question struck Billy's heart. He said goodbye to his friends and decided to follow the group back to the mission. "I'm done with this way of living," he said. Billy Sunday attended services at Pacific Garden Mission every night for the next two weeks.

One night, when Mrs. Clarke issued an invitation to come to the altar, Billy Sunday went, and professed his faith in Jesus Christ.[20] Later, he would tell Sarah Clarke, "I made the great and only decision worth making which committed me to the Christian life. I staggered out of sin into the arms of a Savior."[21] Following his conversion, Billy Sunday eventually left professional baseball and went on to become one of the country's great evangelists leading more than one million people to Christ.

As the couple continued to work together at their mission, it is said that they fell even more deeply in love. On Clarke's sixty-third birthday, he penned a poem to his wife. It read:

> "I've marched along with you, dear wife, / Our steps with knee to knee, / My heart enrapted with you, my dear, / And your warm heart with me; / For thus, dear wife, it ever should, / With married people be."[22]

As Sarah remembered those years, she knew they were difficult, but also eternally valuable. To save money, the couple used public transportation and walked long distances. One night, they took a late train at midnight, then tramped through slush and sleet for two miles to their house. They were weary and bone-chillingly cold. Chicago was being blasted by a terrible storm and they walked through sleet and hail the entire way. When they at last reached their door, Sarah says she felt a dark, ominous presence.

At that same moment, a question pressed upon her heart, "Does it pay?"

"Yes," she emphatically replied. "I'd walk ten miles—or a night—if I could win one soul."

The couple never felt that dark presence in their home again. Said Sarah, "Disappointments have been many, but discouragement never."[23]

After working together for fifteen years, on June 22, 1892, her husband died. Sarah was deeply grieved by the loss, but resolved to carry on the work of the mission to honor him and God.

She commemorated her husband's life with a farewell poem that expressed their love and common goal of service: "In living thus for others, dear, / We've found a solace sweet, / As we have tried to lessen some / The tramp of weary feet; / And caused some aching hearts, I trust. / More cheerfully to beat."[24]

CHAPTER THIRTEEN

Mother of the Mission

The years following George's death may have been sorrowful and lonely, but Sarah pushed on. She filled day after day with her dedication to reaching the lost souls of Chicago. Harry Monroe, one of the mission's converts, was appointed as the new director, but Sarah remained on in her role as the "Mother of the Mission."[25]

She was fully committed to the work. Sarah lived a simple, frugal life, giving every spare penny to the work God set before her. She would often pull out her personal checkbook and cover the bills. On workdays, she would eat a simple lunch of tea and toast at her desk. She walked incredibly long distances rather than spend money on transportation. She lived and breathed the work of God at Pacific Garden Mission. It was said that Sarah and George had only one child, who did not survive long after birth—but in a very real sense, the young men and women who entered the mission became her children. In that sense she was the mother of thousands.[26]

During mission services, Sarah would sit in the front and keep an eye on those who were in attendance. If she saw a man becoming noisy, she would quietly walk back and sit down beside him, placing her arm around his shoulders. "You must be still now, for we want to tell you about Jesus your Savior," Sarah would whisper. Then she would stand and return to the platform.[27]

If the person continued to disrupt the meeting, she would signal for one of the ushers to escort him outside. The mission leaders did not tolerate anyone disturbing the meeting. One day a man came to the mission too inebriated to talk. Before he left, someone slipped a small testament into his pocket next to his whiskey flask. The next day, the man took out the flask and the Bible and saw a note—"From one who is praying for you." This reminded him of the prayers of his mother and he came back to the mission to meet the people who had reached out to him.[28]

Life at the mission was never dull—men and women continued to arrive who were in desperate need of a kind word and God's healing power. When the World's Fair ended, the thousands of people who had been employed for its construction were suddenly laid off and stranded in the city. Homelessness seemed to increase and vagrants were seen sleeping on the streets or under the elevated trains. These same men would wander into the mission services looking for help and hope.

Sarah and her helpers worked overtime. In a very real sense, the mission became her home. In addition to her evenings at the mission, Sarah extended the work of the mission to departments organizing prison work and hospital visitation. She also noted that the first free kindergarten classes in Chicago were held at the mission. For twenty-seven years, almost 10,000 nights, she never missed a single mission service and never mentioned it to anyone.[29] In 1905, someone noticed the extraordinary gift she had given of her faithful service and time and the staff gave her a special party of appreciation.

Sarah Clarke did not always realize the effect she had on each man or woman who came to the mission services, but she extended the same gracious spirit to all. In her quiet way, she extended a respect and dignity to people regardless of their condition. It was this steadfast love that broke through many hardened hearts.

One young woman named Minnie Prouix wrote to Mrs. Clarke—she had been in the county hospital with a nail in her foot. She watched a mission worker visiting the sick. The woman stopped at the bed of a "street girl," prayed with her, and then stooped down and kissed her. Minnie was shocked by such a demonstration of Christ's love and wrote, "That's what opened the door of my heart. If a woman could kiss that Magdalene—all covered with sin—that's the kind of religion I want—and sure enough, I got it."[30]

Sarah remembered one particularly challenging convert: "Jimmy the Rat." Jimmy had grown up in Indiana. His father had hired workers on their farm, and those men had introduced the young boy to opium. He became so addicted that he ran from home and ended up in Chicago, living on the streets. He earned the nickname "Jimmy the Rat" because he would often curl up and sleep on the shelves of the opium den that he frequented.[31]

One night, Jimmy staggered into the mission during an evening service. He looked wild and out of control. Jimmy raised his hands in the middle of the aisle, calling out, "I want somebody to pray for me!" Sarah came quietly, but quickly, down the steps off of the platform. She put her hand on Jimmy's arm and led him up to a front seat. She knelt down, and he dropped to his knees next to her.

"It was like a dream," said Jimmy, later, of that moment. People gathered around him offering prayers and words of encouragement and he felt the "peace of God that passeth all understanding." After his time at the mission, Jimmy went back to Indiana, married, and raised a family. He did not like to talk of the time when he was "Jimmy the Rat"—but his family said that every night he asked God to bless the Pacific Garden Mission.[32]

The mission had a way of producing converts, or "home-grown fruit," who would go on to save many more for Christ. In addition to Billy Sunday, one of the greatest was Mel Trotter, who started more than sixty rescue missions of his own.[33]

Whiskey had been the consuming god of Trotter's life. He had failed miserably to break his addiction to alcohol, finally leaving his home and wife in despair. He said that on the "darkest night of his life" he went to the Pacific Garden Mission and heard the story of God's love. When an invitation was given, Trotter raised his hand for prayer and "the light of God shone in his soul." God radically changed his life that day and he determined to serve Him fully for the rest of his life.[34]

Trotter was just one of thousands who were saved by the faithful, tireless work of Sarah Clarke and others who believed in bringing God's love to the needy of Chicago. Sarah wrote, "Just one glimpse backward to the birthplace of the Old Mission, sends a thrill of thanksgiving for what God hath wrought all these years. As a pebble dropped in the ocean causes a ripple that never ceases to lose its momentum, so Pacific Garden Mission has set in motion influences reaching to the end of the earth."[35]

In 1914, Sarah was in an unusual accident that prevented her from keeping up her pace of work with the "absorbing and consuming passion" of her life.[36] While shopping on State Street, she was caught in a revolving door at one of the department stores. In the weeks that followed, while bed-ridden, she began to write her story of the mission and its converts.

Looking back, Sarah marveled at how God brought the Pacific Garden Mission through many storms. "Its struggles and victories will never be known, until the Recording Angel reveals the secret record," wrote Sarah. "He who marks the sparrow's fall has always shielded us in times of storm."[37]

Sarah Dunn Clarke died in 1918 and was buried in Mt. Greenwood Cemetery in Chicago, Illinois. At last, she was reunited with her husband, George, and saw "face-to-face" the God she had so faithfully served.

One biographer wrote, "unsung and unknown women have the greatest share in pushing on God's work among the lost. A most notable woman of this kind, whose praises are not sounded forth by blare of horns and newspaper notoriety, was Sarah Dunn Clarke. All her tasks were done with great love."[38]

AMANDA SMITH

1837–1915

CHAPTER FOURTEEN

Finding Freedom

A manda tiptoed into the dimly lit room, peering past her mother at the sick girl lying in the bed. Miss Celie's face was pale. Silently, her mother dipped a cloth into the wash basin and wiped the girl's forehead in an attempt to relieve her spiking fever. So intent was Mariam on tending to the child, that she did not hear her young daughter approach.

"Is Miss Celie gonna be okay?" whispered Amanda.

Startled, Mariam jumped and turned toward her daughter. Her face reflected grave concern. "I don't know, child," she said sadly. "Pray with me and ask the good Lord above to heal her. We must pray!"

Gently, she motioned Amanda toward the open door. "Go now," she said. "We must let Miss Celie sleep."

Amanda's mother, Mariam Berry, was a slave in the home of the Greens. Celie was the teenage daughter of her mother's owners, who managed a small farm in Maryland. Mariam had met her husband, Samuel, because he was a slave at the neighboring farm. Although they were not free to live together, they considered themselves fortunate to be owned by people who treated them kindly. Recently, Samuel had done a great favor for his owner, who had in turn allowed him to purchase his freedom. Now, he was saving up to purchase back the "ownership" of his wife, Mariam, and their five children.

Mariam especially loved caring for Miss Celie, who was now struggling to fight off typhoid fever, an illness that had already stolen so many lives. What began as a simple stomachache had quickly escalated to a serious illness. The doctor had ordered complete bed rest, but did not seem encouraging. Mariam comforted the girl by singing spirituals. "Pray for me, Mariam," said Celie. And Mariam prayed. Miss Celie had given her life to Jesus the year before, much to the concern of her parents who were not religious people.

When Mrs. Green came in to check on her daughter, Celie opened her eyes. "Mama," she said, each word an effort. "I want you to free Mariam and the children."

"Quiet now," said her mother, dismissing the girl's request. "Go back to sleep."

Again the next day, Celie repeated her plea, "Mama, you must free Mariam and the children. Give them to Samuel."

Miss Celie's condition did not improve. Finally, when the family had gathered to say their final goodbyes, Celie spoke once more. "Please," she insisted, her voice shaking with effort. "I want you to free Mariam and the children. Their family should be reunited. It is what God would want." Tearfully, her mother nodded. Miss Celie's dying wish would be honored, and the Berry family would be set free.

As Mariam began to sing an old hymn, Miss Celie passed into heaven's gates. Amanda watched from the corner of the room, barely realizing how the dying girl's final wish had changed her life forever.[1]

Amanda Berry considered herself blessed to have parents who believed in God and who demonstrated a calm and steady faith. They had believed, for many years, that God would deliver them from slavery. Each night the children were taught to pray before bed, and Samuel and Mariam, both of whom could read, would teach them from the Bible. Food was scarce, but they never went hungry. Supper was sometimes a simple meal of milk and mush.

At age eight, Amanda attended her first school, taught by the daughter of a Methodist minister. It was a little private school and the teacher was pretty and kind. She taught Amanda to spell—and, although Amanda was only able to attend for a few months because the school closed, she taught herself to read at home by cutting letters out of newspapers and arranging them to form words.[2]

After Miss Celie's death, the family moved to Pennsylvania where her father rented land from a man named John Lowe, a local judge. Many of the men, including Mr. Lowe, were known for their antislavery views.[3]

In Pennsylvania, at age thirteen, she attended school again, but the distance of the school from their home, nearly five miles, made attending each day a burden. She only attended for two weeks.[4] Instead, Amanda began domestic work, which would be her primary occupation for most of her adult life. Her first job was working for a woman named Mrs. Latimer, a Southern widow who had five children. Working in a private home left Amanda isolated for most of her day, and she longed for the company of others. She decided to attend a church.

She could hear the music as she approached the small country church, and Amanda slipped quietly inside the door. She took a seat in the very last pew and nervously looked to make sure the other worshipers wouldn't ask her to leave, but they continued to sing. The music was beautiful and reminded Amanda of her grandmother. Then the preacher began to speak. He spoke of sinners and a loving God. He asked each person to examine their soul to see if God was calling.

Amanda sensed that God was calling her. He wanted her, a simple, poor, black girl, to serve Him. The thought overwhelmed her and tears welled up in her eyes, her chin quivering with emotion. Suddenly, she felt a woman's arm around her small, shaking shoulders. She looked up to see one of the speakers, Miss Mary Bloser, sitting on the pew next to her. Miss Bloser put her arm around Amanda, and, through her own tears, asked her if she would like to pray. Amanda nodded. "Oh how she prayed!" remembered Amanda. "I was ignorant, but I prayed the best I could. I went home and resolved I would be the Lord's and live for him."[5]

Even though Amanda had been raised by godly parents and grandparents, she still struggled with doubts about God and her faith. She remembered one time when she was walking with her aunt across a long bridge. They stopped to gaze out over the water and marvel at the day's beauty. Her aunt remarked, "How wonderful how God has created everything." Amanda hesitated. Looking at her aunt, she said, "How do you know there is a God?" Her aunt turned in surprise. Staring at Amanda, she stamped her foot, and reprimanded the young girl. "Don't you ever speak to me again. Anybody that has as good a Christian mother as you had and was raised as you have been to speak so to me!" Her aunt's response startled Amanda. She said, "And, God broke the snare. I felt it. I felt deliverance from that hour."[6]

Amanda saw her parents live out their faith in dramatic ways. Their home was one of the main stations on the Underground Railroad that ran from the South to the North and helped slaves escape to freedom. Her father was renting property from an antislavery man, and the other farms immediately surrounding were owned by men with similar beliefs. However, life was not easy for black men and women in this time period. Even for those who were not living in slavery, the ability to earn money and to move freely was severely limited.

Her father worked long and hard in the fields. After a day of hard labor, he would be awakened at night by an escaped slave. Sometimes he would only sleep about two hours, then be awakened at midnight and walk fifteen to twenty miles to take a slave to a safer place. She remembered groups of white men pounding on their door in the middle of the night and then searching the premises for escaped slaves. Again and again, her father risked his health and life to save the lives of others.

In 1854, at age seventeen, she decided to get married. Her parents were concerned, for Amanda was still very young. Her husband was Calvin Devine. And although she was in love when they first married, that feeling faded quickly as she realized he was a drunkard. The couple had two children, the first dying shortly after birth. The second was a little girl named Mazie.

Life was difficult, and Amanda continued to serve as a domestic servant to earn enough money to keep her child fed and clothed. Calvin left to serve in the Civil War and was killed. Amanda became a young widow.[7] Even in those difficult years, she continued to feel a strong sense of God's presence. Her life was simple and she worked long hours in other people's homes, yet Amanda wrote:

> I found out that it was not necessary to be a nun or be isolated away off in some deep retirement to have communion with Jesus; but, though your hands are employed in doing your daily business; it is no bar to the soul's communion with Jesus. Many times over my wash-tub and ironing table, and while making my bed and sweeping my house and washing my dishes I have had some of the richest blessings.[8]

In 1863, she married a second time to James Smith, a man who told her that he wanted to be a minister. They talked a great deal about God and about how they could serve together in ministry. But soon after they were married, Amanda realized she had been deceived. Her husband admitted, "I was afraid to tell you what was really in my heart. I was afraid you would not marry me."[9]

The couple moved to New York where James took a position in a hotel where he boarded and worked. Amanda lived with Mazie and their other children in a small apartment, serving nearby as a cook. Money was tight, and she was lonesome. She was a young black mother in a city dominated by white people. At times the racial tensions were overwhelming to her. She clung to the Bible verse:

There is neither Jew nor Greek, there is neither bond nor free man, there is neither male nor female, for ye are all one in Christ Jesus. (Galatians 3:28)

Amanda said, "I never understood that text before. And as I looked at white people that I had always seemed to be afraid of, now they looked so small. The great mountain had become a mole hill."[10]

One day Amanda was at home cleaning and caring for her children. She had cleaned the room and was filling a little basin with warm water to give her baby Will a bath. Her daughter Mazie was getting ready to go to school when she called out to her mom. "Oh Ma, look at Will."

Amanda looked at the little baby who had just a moment before been playing and smiling. Now, he lay stiffened in some sort of seizure with foam at his mouth. Quickly, she stripped off his clothes and put him in the bath water. "I did not know how I did it," remembered Amanda. "God kept me so still in my soul."

He soon came out of his spasm when she put him in the warm water. The baby opened his eyes, and looked at Amanda. "Mama," he said, reaching out to her.

Amanda gasped and hugged the baby close. Will seemed all right then, so she put him down for a nap. He slept and ate, but she sensed that he was still not right.

"There was no one to call," said Amanda. Finally, she dressed and took him to a doctor for medicine. The prescription cost $1.50 and she only had two dollars. With fifty cents left, they returned home. But the medicine did not do any good. In another few days, the baby stiffened again in another spasm. For weeks, Will continued to decline, and Amanda stayed up with him around the clock. This tiny baby was special to her. He was the brightest of her children, and, when he was just three days old, she had prayed and dedicated his life to God. How could God take him now? She kept praying and praying: "Thy will be done." It was the cry of her soul.

On the final night of Will's life, she felt that her hope was drying up. She sent for her husband, James, but he said he couldn't come to help her. He had no money and wasn't feeling well himself. At two in the morning, she held Will in her arms as he passed into the arms of Jesus. "God seemed to dry up my tears with joy. Oh, the greatness of His peace that passeth understanding."[11]

Amanda sat in silence. Her baby was gone. Her husband had deserted her. Her other children needed to be fed. She had to go to work. She had no money, just fifty cents left to her name.

She packed a bag, intending to go to her former employer to ask if she could earn enough money to bury her child. Suddenly, a knock came at the door. It was a dear friend. Her friend looked into Amanda's sad, desperate eyes, and said, "I heard your baby is dead."

Amanda replied, "Yes."

Her friend said, "If twenty dollars will help you, I can let you have it."

Amanda said, in that moment, "I saw God, and wept."[12]

For Amanda, a former slave, bought with a price, then bought once again with the Lord's salvation, her life seemed fraught with worry and despair. Just a few months after losing Will, her husband, James, would die of stomach cancer. She would be twice a widow, a mother, and completely alone. How could God use one small woman with so much to bear?

CHAPTER FIFTEEN

From Camp Meetings to Africa

The huge canvas tent was filled with worshipers, a small taste of heaven's glory on earth. Fiery preaching called sinners to be saved and for the coldhearted to open their souls to the power of the Holy Spirit. The old hymns were sung with an energy that filled the tent, the groaning organ music barely audible over the harmony of enthusiastic voices singing praises to God.

Amanda's heart was full. She had been asked to attend the Holiness Camp Meeting in Maryland. In 1870, these camp meetings were not new events. They had started in the South as a way to energize believers and reach the lost. Many towns did not have their own churches or depended on circuit preachers who would make an occasional visit to the area. These camp meetings were a key to revival in the hearts of the faithful and would later grow into full-fledged evangelistic campaigns led by men like D. L. Moody.

In the mid-1800s, the meetings spread to the North. Some were attended by as many as 25,000 people who would stay for days in makeshift lodging. Since Amanda struggled to have enough money for food and shelter, she didn't see a way to attend the meetings. She considered hiring herself out to clean cabins and tents, but a good friend told her she could stay in their room—so she could attend *and* participate in the meeting. The Holiness Camp Meetings filled Amanda with tremendous joy. As she listened to testimonies from Christians young and old, she felt a beautiful sense of communion with fellow believers.

On this evening, the leader was asking the congregation to give what they could to support the cause. A basket passed from one person to the next to collect the offering. Amanda noticed a wealthy white woman sitting a few rows ahead of her. The woman was wearing a very fine, fashionable, leghorn straw bonnet trimmed with black lace, the kind found in only the most expensive boutiques. Around her shoulders was an elegant black shawl.

Amanda thought to herself, "That woman should give *twenty* dollars because she is so rich. Oh, I wish I had twenty dollars like her to give."

Immediately, she felt the conviction of the Holy Spirit. Speaking to her heart, God gently urged, "*You* give that two dollars." She did.[13]

At this first camp meeting, and then for many others, Amanda Smith began to minister. She would sing and testify and read from the Scriptures. People were so moved by her testimony that they paid her expenses to participate in revival meetings. At each turn, God met her financial and personal needs—never far in advance or in abundance—but just enough to meet that moment's needs.

It was during this time period that Amanda decided to wear the simple Quaker bonnet and dress for which she became known. She had always admired the simple style of the Friends, and appreciated their devotion to God and their desire to avoid vanity. She said, "I wanted to be a consistent, downright, outright Christian." Not only did her simple outfit eliminate pride, but it kept the audience's focus on God and His Word—not on herself.[14]

In the 1870s, the equal participation of a black woman in church or public life was unusual—even in areas where they were considered "free." Despite the fact that she had left slavery many years ago, Amanda still faced discrimination and poor treatment in public places. She was aware that she should keep "her place" and not go where she was not wanted.

In Philadelphia, she wanted to attend Bible readings held by well-known Bible teacher Hannah Whitall Smith, but she wasn't sure if colored people would be allowed to attend the meeting. On her way, she happened to sit near Robert Pearson Smith, Hannah's husband. He asked her, "Are you Amanda Smith?" He then proceeded to take the seat next to her and did not show any embarrassment at being seen in the company of a colored woman. "How real and kind and true he was," said Amanda.[15]

He asked her if she planned to attend his wife's meetings and told her that she would be very welcome. However, when she arrived in front of the prestigious address, she was still nervous. Amanda prayed to God to give her courage to attend the white gathering. "I always tried to avoid anything like pushing myself or going where I was not wanted," she explained. When she arrived, a woman at the door told her that the meeting was full and that there were many wealthy women who needed places to sit and that maybe she could come back another time.

Humiliated, Amanda stepped back and took a deep breath. Despite her personal fears, she felt convinced that God wanted her to attend that meeting. She entered again, slipped quietly inside, and stood at the back.

Immediately following the meeting, before she could slip away unnoticed, a finely dressed woman approached her. "Are you Amanda Smith? Why didn't you sing for us? Why didn't you speak?" Amanda felt convicted by her lack of confidence in God's protection. She said, "I was not so well known then and many people were shy of me, and are yet. But, I belong to Royalty and am well acquainted with the King of Kings and am better known and better understood among the great family above than I am on earth."[16]

So, Amanda Berry Smith considered herself truly "free" even before slavery was finally abolished.

In 1872, at age thirty-five, she felt God's tugging at her heart to go to Africa. Since she was a little girl, her parents had told her stories about that land. She had heard tales of lions and other wild animals. She had been shown a book that had large pictures of Africans in their native costumes and living in huts. At one of the camp meetings she attended, missionaries spoke about God's work in India, China, Japan, and South America. Why, Amanda wondered, didn't they talk about Africa? Who was reaching the African people?

She felt another one of God's nudgings on her life: to go somewhere that she had never before dreamed of actually going. She prayed, "Lord, Africa's need is so great, and I cannot go, though I would like to. But Thou Knowest I have no education, and I do not understand the geography, so I would not know how to travel."[17]

After the meeting, life continued as usual, and Amanda traveled across the United States to meeting after meeting. Friends bought her a home in Philadelphia, and she began to put down roots. In Boston, she attended an evangelistic meeting held by the great preacher Dwight Lyman Moody. He spoke of work in England where he would be preaching at the Keswick Convention. Several women said they were attending and invited her to go with them. Amanda was frightened. She had never traveled abroad. Although her daughter was now grown (sadly, none of her other children lived to adulthood), she was reluctant to leave the States.

At Moody's meeting, the preacher asked them to turn to Philippians 4:19, "My God shall supply all your need according to his riches in glory by Christ Jesus." God would supply her needs—all of them—her financial worries and personal worries should be set aside since she was the daughter of the King.

Amanda agreed to go. She went home and packed her trunk and boarded the Steamer Ohio for England. She was the only black woman on the ship, among a great many white, aristocratic passengers. The captain took her aside and befriended her. He said since there was no preacher aboard, maybe she could read from the gospel of John and lead them in a hymn. Suddenly, the atmosphere onboard ship changed, and the people she had once feared became her friends.

In England, she was asked to sing and speak. She was a novelty as a black woman and a former slave. As many as six hundred people at a time would attend those meetings.[18] She was able to attend and speak at a great many meetings, and once again heard Mr. Moody in Edinburgh. In 1879, she received an invitation by Lucy Drake to travel to India. They would go overland and visit Paris, Florence, and Rome. With each step, she felt God's leading despite her initial reluctance. She was also awed that she was able to visit such incredible places: cathedrals, museums, even the pyramids. As a poor black girl, she had never dreamed that she would have these opportunities.

Sister Smith knelt on the grass and began to pray. She turned her face—smiling—to the sky and poured out her soul. The crowd became very still—transfixed by her appearance—and did not even whisper. It was as if they were in the midst of a church.

In October, they sailed to Bombay. Amanda would travel and speak, opening God's Word and also sharing her views on temperance. She met Salvation Army lassies who were blessed of God and doing his work in desperate conditions.

One pastor spoke of her ministry in Calcutta. Many had come to listen to the former slave speak. They stood in the open square in the heart of the city. Crowds gathered to listen. In the past few nights, Christian preachers had been treated roughly, but Amanda was not afraid. The bishop, standing to her side, noticed a group of men and boys gathering, moving toward the square with loud cries and threats.

He wrote of the occurrence,

Sister Smith knelt on the grass and began to pray. She turned her face—smiling—to the sky and poured out her soul. The crowd became very still—transfixed by her appearance—and did not even whisper. It was as if they were in the midst of a church.[19]

She was sometimes touched by the pictures of the misery which she saw around her, but never became hopeless. She was of cheerful temperament, it is true, but aside from personal feeling, she always possessed a buoyant hope and an overcoming faith which made it easy for her to believe, that the Savior, whom she loved and served, really intended to save and transform India.[20]

Amanda's world was broadened by her travels through Europe and India, but God was not finished with her yet. She was soon asked to travel to the continent she had only dreamed about: Africa. Before she left, she wrote to Mazie, praying that God would continue to lead her daughter in marriage and education.

In Africa, the people's educational, spiritual, and physical needs overwhelmed her. She wished her supporters in America could be with her and see the need for books and medicine. She never asked for money—she had never operated that way—but would only make her requests known to God. Weeks went by without any funds arriving. She would open envelopes with letters but no money. She continued to pray. Two weeks later, she received a letter from Ireland, including a five-pound note. Then came another letter from America, with five dollars. God showed her that when she depended fully on Him, that He would provide.

She would travel from place to place by canoe. She visited schools and mission stations. There was a great need for books and education. She met many young men and women who did not know how to read. The circumstances frustrated her, yet she believed that God could work: "How often I have stood still and seen God overrule things of man's device, and work His sovereign will."[21]

As she traveled and met people in all regions, she observed that the Africans often seemed to believe more in the devil than in God. They would pray and set dishes of rice and fish out at night to give the devil a good meal. They felt like if they kept on good terms with him that he would give them good crops and keep away sickness. She saw a great need for the missionaries to continue to preach God's Word.

She was upset by the conditions facing African women who would marry at age thirteen or fourteen, sometimes even younger. She mourned the fact that they belonged to a man from the moment they were born. She saw infants just a few months old wearing betrothal jewels. Women were treated as second-class citizens, walking behind men and carrying the burdens. "No matter how tired she is," wrote Amanda, "the man never thinks of bringing her a jar of water to cook his supper with and neither will the boys."[22]

If the woman married a cruel man, there was little hope for her. Some missionaries would "buy" a girl and pay her dowry for $20 to $25 just to save her from a miserable life. Amanda wrote, "When I first went to Africa, I saw there was much to do, and I felt I could do little."[23]

While she was there, she adopted a young boy named Bob. His parents wanted her to take him along with her and educate him to be a missionary and a doctor. Amanda cared for the boy as if he was one of her own, sending him to school, teaching him the Bible and English. He loved her almost as his own "mama."[24]

In 1890, she left Sierra Leone to journey back to England and then home to the United States. It had been many years since she had left and her health was suffering. "I was so tired of holding on and trying to keep up. It seemed to me the Lord had done all I asked Him, and now all I had to do was the little I could do for myself. . . . I went to Africa at [God's] bidding, and did not leave until I was sure I had his sanction."[25]

Back home again, she could not help wonder what task God would give her the courage to tackle next.

CHAPTER SIXTEEN

Caring for Chicago's Orphans

E
verybody in Chicago was excited about the soon-approaching World's Fair. For the past several years, construction had been bustling on the lake shore site as workers cleared land, built huge structures for exhibits, and even laid tracks for the railroads that would bring supplies. Thousands of workers had migrated to the city in hopes of employment. The city's population and landscape were changing. Skyscrapers were being built as Chicago reached higher and farther outward.

It had been three years since Amanda had returned from Africa, and urban life stood in stark contrast to the rural plains of Africa. For several years she lived in New York and New Jersey. While staying with friends on the East Coast, she was asked to write her life's story. She was intimidated by the task, not viewing herself as a writer, nor her life of any particular importance. But she decided to record God's working in her life as a gift to others.

"I pray that many of my own people will be led to a more full consecration, and that the Spirit of the Lord may come upon some of the younger women who have talent, and who have had better opportunities than I have ever had, and so must do better work for the Master."

She wrote:

And now I close the last chapter of this little book, which has been such a task to one so unskilled in work of this kind. There has been no attempt to show a dash of rhetoric or intellectual ability, but just the simple story of God's dealings with a worm. If, after all, no one should be brought nearer to God, and to a deeper consecration, I shall be sadly disappointed; for my whole object and wish is that God will make it a blessing to all who may read it.

Amanda continued:

I pray that many of my own people will be led to a more full consecration, and that the Spirit of the Lord may come upon some of the younger women who have talent, and who have had better opportunities than I have ever had, and so must do better work for the Master; so that when I have fallen in the battle, and can do no more, they may take up the standard and bear it on, with the inscription deeply engraven on heart and life, "Without holiness, no man shall see the Lord."[26]

Amanda moved to Chicago where she published her book and continued her work as a speaker for the temperance cause. It was an exciting time in Chicago with the approach of the World's Fair. She became further acquainted with Frances Willard, an outspoken advocate for suffrage and the rights of women. Willard and the Chicago Women's Christian Temperance Union (WCTU) were warning people about the dangers of alcohol, but they were also lobbying to protect the rights of women and children. Amanda joined Frances and many others in the WCTU in speaking to the Christian and political issues of the day.

Returning to Chicago also brought her in contact, once again, with evangelist D. L. Moody. His school to train Christian workers was growing. One of Moody's vice presidents, Turlington W. Harvey, was involved in planning a temperance community on the South Side of Chicago. As a member of the WCTU, Amanda was interested.

Harvey, Illinois, as it was to be named, would be designed as a planned temperance community. An 1892 article explained that the town would be designed as an escape from the evils of the city. It would be a town where "no intoxicating liquors are bought or sold, no property being sold without a prohibition clause in each deed."[27] The location, just twenty miles south of Chicago, could be easily reached by railroad lines. Moody and Harvey planned to use the World's Fair as an opportunity to promote the new town as a moral alternative to the dangers and immoral activities of Chicago. A special train between the fair and Harvey would allow visitors to see this special city that was under construction.

Harvey, thought Amanda, would be the perfect place for an orphanage. Since returning to the United States, Amanda Smith had continued to participate in many forms of service, but God began to lay it upon her heart to establish a home for destitute black children. She wanted to raise funds for an orphanage, and decided to locate this endeavor in the "Christian" town of Harvey.

She spoke of her project to everyone she met—at churches, temperance meetings, and camp meetings. People began to donate . . . slowly. But even though funds were scarce, Amanda refused to give up this vision that she believed God had called her to accomplish. Just as she had done years before in Africa, Amanda prayed for God to send the needed funds.

In 1893, Amanda was named as a National Evangelist in the Women's Christian Temperance Union and they helped promote her plans to build the orphanage in their national magazine, *The Union Signal*. At their world convention in Boston, Amanda was called to the platform to sing and introduced as "God's image carved in ebony."[28]

African-American women in Chicago were significant financial and prayerful supporters of Amanda Smith's work. From 1890 to 1920, many of these women had formed Colored Women's Clubs across the country and there were more than 150 clubs in Chicago.[29]

With the rising middle class of African Americans, these women wanted to improve the living conditions for black families and children. They were involved in forming kindergartens, nurseries, social settlements, and orphanages, and worked to defend the rights of working women and the elderly. They were involved in political issues like suffrage and discrimination. The clubs also played a significant role in helping organizations like Amanda Smith's Home for Dependent and Orphaned Girls. To raise money, club women held plays, musicals, raffles, picnics, and balls.[30]

In Harvey, Amanda began a small newspaper called *The Helper*, to publicize her orphanage. It described the home as a place for the "care, education, and industrial training of orphaned, destitute, needy children, and especially those of colored parentage."[31]

Amanda approached major donors as well, and received an important contribution from Julius Rosenwald, president of Sears, Roebuck and Company. In 1895, she had enough initial funds raised to purchase her first property for six thousand dollars. At the dedication, in June of 1899, a local paper reported that "in a wild storm of wind and rain, large company was gathered at North Harvey, Illinois, for the opening of the Orphanage."[32]

Despite all of the hardships and the long wait, Amanda had once again seen God provide a way. The home began with an endowment of $288 and five orphans. By 1910, the home had grown to thirty-three children. Amanda was able to live to see her dream become a reality. She had traveled far from the home she once knew, to Africa and back again, and was now able to provide a home to children in need.

In 1912, at the age of seventy-five, Amanda's health began to rapidly decline, and she finally decided to slow down from her busy life of ministry and retire. A wealthy supporter, George Sebring, purchased a cottage for her in Sebring, Florida, where she stayed to recover. Amanda wrote, "I told the Board that they must get someone to take charge of the work. I was not able to carry it any longer. . . . I am already past my 76th birthday, Jan.

23rd. Some kind, white friends have given me a home here during my life time, will look after my other needs so that I am relieved of the care and anxiety."[33]

Amanda Smith remained in Florida until her death on February 24, 1915. Her friend and donor, George Sebring, arranged for her body to be returned to Chicago by train—with a group of white clergymen accompanying her casket to the train in Florida. She was buried with honor and still remembered today as one of the great women in African-American history.

On March 1, 1915, she was buried near Harvey, Illinois, in "one of the largest funerals in the history of the African American community in Chicago."[34]

CHAPTER SEVENTEEN

Women in Missions

—————

When we think of a single woman missionary, we may picture her with a long skirt, brimmed hat, and laced-up boots, bravely carrying her Bible and folding organ into jungle villages. While not every missionary fit that description, it is true that many missionaries leaving the United States for foreign lands at the turn-of-the-century were female *and* single.

For years, women had heard about the adventures of male missionaries and their wives. In her book *The Gospel of Gentility*, Jane Hunter says that many women were only able to enter the field by giving money in support. A great number of women's "cent" and "mite" societies saved every extra penny to support foreign missions. They also enjoyed hearing reports from the field.[1]

Hunter writes, "Female supporters thrilled to the courage and heroism of young missionary women who accompanied their husbands to the jungles of Asia and Africa, and who suffered and perished nobly there."[2] Ruth A. Tucker and Walter Liefeld, in their book *Daughters of the Church*, describe this trend. "The one area of church ministry above all others that captured the imaginations of women during the late nineteenth and early twentieth centuries was that of foreign missions."[3]

But the Civil War, which brought significant changes to women's education, also made the way for women to leave for the foreign field . . . unmarried. "Prior to the Civil War, the sending boards considered single service for women an impropriety, and single women who sought to serve met with scant encouragement."[4]

According to Hunter, by 1890, married and single women made up as much as 60 percent of the missions force![5] This increased interest in missions meant that the number of women who were actively supporting missionaries grew as well. By 1915, there were more than three million women who belonged to church missionary societies.[6]

Elisabeth Elliot, author, missionary, and wife of the martyred Jim Elliot, wrote, "Far from being excluded, women constituted the majority of foreign missionaries."[7] One reason that the number of *single* female missionaries was increasing was that available single men were scarce. In addition, women who were committed to God's work often turned down proposals if their suitor wasn't equally spiritually minded or did not share their commitment to missions.

One such woman was missionary Lottie Moon (1840–1912). Lottie, a tiny four foot three inches tall, was determined to leave her home of Virginia to go to China as a missionary. She turned down a marriage proposal from a Confederate army chaplain named Crawford Toy before she left for China. While Crawford *was* interested in both missionary work *and* in marriage, Lottie discovered that his Christian faith did not match her own. Crawford believed in evolution—and that initial disagreement eventually pushed the couple apart.

Once, after being asked if she had ever been in love, Moon answered, "Yes, but God had first claim on my life, and since the two conflicted, there could be no question about the result."[8]

Some single female missionaries proclaimed vows of celibacy. Like Evangeline Booth, who decided early that she could best serve God as a single woman, missionary Amy Carmichael (1867–1951) also proclaimed her decision to never marry. She wrote, "On this day many years ago, I went away alone to a cave. . . . I had feelings of fear about the future. That was why I went there—to be alone with God. The devil kept on whispering.

'It is all right now, but what about afterwards? You are going to be very lonely.' Carmichael went on to spend fifty-five years in India without any type of furlough, working with children and rescuing girls from temple prostitution.[9]

Women in foreign lands were allowed access to people and areas never before infiltrated by men. Because of her gender, Amy had a unique opportunity to interact with and then rescue temple girls from prostitution. So close was Amy to these female orphans, that when she died, the children she had loved and devoted her life to, put a bird bath over her grave with the word "Amma," which means "mother."

In China, when female missionaries were allowed to arrive during the second half of the nineteenth century, they focused their efforts on issues related to the health and well-being of women. They often were involved in legal reform. Female missionaries in China worked to abolish the oppressive practice of female foot binding, much to the anger of the government.

The students who came to Moody Bible Institute in the late 1800s and early 1900s had missionary service deeply embedded on their minds and hearts. Some, like Mary McLeod Bethune, were turned away from various missions boards due to race or gender, but many others were able to go and serve. Many early graduates left for places across the country and for faraway lands like China, Turkey, Africa, and Persia.

A letter from Miss Alma Benedict, one of the early graduates of Moody's school, reported on her mission work in Africa. It was published in an 1892 issue of *The Institute Tie*. Alma wrote, "Some of them felt it to be a trifle venturesome for me to go to the country so soon, where I would have to eat native food, largely, and live in native style . . . no white woman has ever ventured it before . . . but we felt assured that it was the Lord's will." She ends her report with words of assurance, certainly felt by other women missionaries: "I doubt if I could be so happy anywhere else in the world, for this is where my Father has placed me."[10]

VIRGINIA ASHER

❦

1869–1937

CHAPTER EIGHTEEN

Women at the World's Fair

It was July 1893, and the Midway Plaisance of the Chicago World's Fair was crowded with visitors. Men, women, and children swept through the central corridor with the force of a violently rushing river current. The women evangelists, assigned to work the Midway, could barely stand up to the onslaught of people pressing forward to gape at the sights and wonders.

Virginia Asher pulled a delicately embroidered handkerchief from the pocket of her long skirt and wiped the sweat from her brow. It was an unusually hot and humid summer day in Chicago, and the wind off Lake Michigan was quiet for once, failing to provide any sort of relief. Her long sleeves, high necked white cotton blouse, and dark sweeping skirt did little to make her more comfortable.

Despite her discomfort, she smiled at her friend, who stood just steps away. They were tired, yes, but they believed in the importance of their mission. Virginia was one of twelve young female missionaries selected by evangelist Dwight Lyman Moody to represent Christ and the church at the Chicago World's Fair. Just one year earlier, in 1892, *The Institute Tie* reported, "For months past, nothing has occupied a position of such importance in the eyes of Chicagoans as the World's Fair."[1]

For Christians, the fair represented a chance to reach thousands of people with the good news of the gospel. The article urged people to consider "the opportunities for doing good and for testifying of Christ." Although only twenty-four, Virginia was already an experienced evangelist with Moody's Chicago church. While many questioned his decision to place young women in such an unseemly environment, Moody felt that their presence set an important example to society, contrasting "moral" women with the "heathen" environment of the fair.[2]

Evangelists recognized that the fair was an incredible opportunity. By mid-July, as many as 100,000 people were arriving in Chicago each day.[3] They came to see new technology, like the first moving pictures, the first zipper, and the first automatic dishwasher. They tasted new brands such as Aunt Jemima, Cracker Jack, and Juicy Fruit.[4] At nighttime, visitors witnessed more electric lights than they had ever seen in one place. The unnatural glow made some fair goers feel like they had "a sudden vision of Heaven."[5]

But most spectacular of all the sights was an enormous rotating steel wheel designed by George Ferris—a structure meant to surpass the Eiffel Tower presented by France for the Paris Exposition in 1889. Despite people's fears that the fragile looking creation would not bear their weight, the Ferris wheel quickly became the most popular attraction at the fair. In the first week, more than sixty thousand tickets were sold, even while many debated the safety of a wheel lifting people 264 feet into the sky.[6]

Virginia and the other women assigned to the fair stood in the shadow of the great wheel. The attraction was located on the Midway Plaisance, which had quickly become the most popular area of the fair. The *Chicago Tribune* questioned the "ethnological" values of the exhibits that included camel and donkey rides, but also more scandalous exhibits like belly dancers.

Of these, in particular, evangelists like Moody did not approve.[7] The fair inspired both admiration and moral outrage among Chicagoans. A great debate had arisen about whether or not the fair should be open on Sundays. Even more controversy had taken place over the questionable content of some of the exhibits.

Despite these issues, the fair was so compelling that people continued to travel from extreme distances to reach the Windy City. One woman, Mrs. Lucille Rodney, from Texas, reportedly walked thirteen hundred miles along railroad tracks to reach the spectacle.[8]

The fair brought good and bad things to Chicago. While hotels and businesses experienced profits, the sanitation services could not accommodate the increased waste. Along with visitors came criminals, and many were arrested for theft and pickpocketing. Also arriving were workers, men and women, who became caught up in the wicked ways of the city. It was for these souls that Virginia's heart was burdened.

Virginia Asher loved the city and desperately wanted to bring the love of Jesus to those in need. She was born in Chicago, as Virginia Healey, to Irish Catholic parents. As a young girl, she was invited to meetings at the Moody Church where Dr. R. A. Torrey was serving as pastor.

One day, the pastor gave an invitation to accept Christ as Savior. His words resonated with young Virginia and she experienced the profound moving of the love of God in her heart. An older woman, Miss Jean Drake, noticing the effect the pastor's words were having on the girl, came and sat down next to Virginia, putting her arms around her. As Miss Drake told the girl about Jesus, she had no idea that her words would light a fire in Virginia's heart that would shine for years to come.[9]

At the same meeting, a boy named William Asher also accepted Christ. Together, they joined a church program that trained young people to serve God. They did not know each other very well—but both became members of the Moody Church. Virginia, in particular, was "eager to try any task."[10] She had a beautiful singing voice and joined the choir as a contralto.

When Mr. Moody visited the church and called for volunteer workers, Virginia raised her hand eagerly. Moody smiled and, even though Virginia was one of the youngest to volunteer, he assigned her to help with outdoor evangelism. It was here that she began to use her gift of singing for God. Her beautiful voice and calm demeanor led many lost souls to the Savior.[11] For Virginia, these moments were a turning point in her life. Reaching the lost, she recognized, was what she was called to do.

In addition to her beautiful voice, Virginia herself was quite attractive. In her teen years, she had many young men pursuing her—and no doubt frustrated by her fixation on the church and serving God. She had no time to get serious with any of them. William, by that point, had become interested in Virginia, but he felt he could not compete with her suitors. His heart ached "for fear one of them might win her."[12]

Like Virginia, William Asher had also grown up in Chicago. His parents, Scottish immigrants, owned a bakery on Clark Street where many of Chicago's urban missionaries would gather.[13] Perhaps it was as a child, listening to the workers talk of their work in rescue missions, saloons, and brothels, when William felt his heart tug toward ministry.

Although he began working in the railways, every spare moment was used to participate in evangelizing with others from Mr. Moody's church. One day, he heard that Virginia was considering leaving Chicago to pursue further Bible education at Moody's Northfield, Massachusetts, school. At that moment, William knew he had to declare his feelings. William made his move and "casting discretion to the winds" began his pursuit of Virginia. His persistence paid off, and the eighteen-year-old agreed to become his bride. They married just before Christmas: December 14, 1887.[14]

Virginia loved being married to William—and found that their common desire to serve God drew them closer together than she had even imagined. While money was scarce, Virginia would save some coins here and there from their weekly allotment. At the end of their first year, in what she called "love in a cottage," she surprised her husband with one hundred dollars that she had tucked away.[15]

Five years later as Virginia pressed tracts into the hands of people passing by at the World's Fair, she had time to think about the strange ways God had directed her life. Certainly she had not expected to be standing there, with these other women, amongst the crowds of humanity. As a woman passing by pushed a pram, her tiny baby crying and wriggling for attention, Virginia offered her a tract and a wistful smile. She gazed for just a moment at the mother and child before quickly averting her eyes.

While those first days of marriage had been wonderful, life had not always been kind to the young couple. Virginia and William had lost their first child who died shortly after birth. She remembered how carefully they had prepared for the arrival of a new life in their little home. She had prepared the nursery and sewn small gowns for the baby's layette, adding embroidered touches to the trim. When tragedy struck, all of those things had been quietly packed away, but another child had not come. Perhaps to be a mother was not her lot in life.

Virginia prayed each day that God would fill that empty void in her heart. William shared her struggle, but not in the same way. Yet she continued to put her trust in God. If He had closed that door, Virginia thought, surely He can open another. Even if she was never meant to be a mother, she was determined to find joy and contentment in serving her Savior.

As the young mother and child moved down the Midway and finally moved out of sight, Virginia turned back to the task at hand. She offered a warm smile and a gospel tract to a fair worker carrying a crate of oranges.

"Excuse me, sir. Would you like to hear about the plan God has for your life?"

CHAPTER NINETEEN

The Fate of Fallen Women

Virginia walked into the opulent parlor. The heady scent of floral perfume filled the air. Thick velvet burgundy drapes adorned the walls and windows. Potted ferns, plush oriental carpets, and gilded picture frames added to the dramatic formal atmosphere. However, Virginia was not paying a call to a wealthy Chicago philanthropist. No, she was visiting the infamous Chicago brothel named the Everleigh Club.

One of the Everleigh sisters had sent for her, asking if she would stop by the house and pray with one of their girls who was very ill. Virginia kindly greeted Ada and Minna, the club's owners. She was there to give comfort to the person in need. Although the sisters did not agree with her religious convictions, they found a friend in Virginia Asher as a kind and compassionate servant of God. They knew that she came, not to judge, but to help them.

Virginia was beloved by "fallen women" and the madams who ran houses of prostitution. She was often called in to read and pray with the sick, write letters to parents, dress wounds, and whisper words of peace to the dying. She was called an "angel of mercy" and a friend to these women who society had rejected. Said one friend, "This pure, white-souled woman brought Christ to many such sinful surroundings."[16]

Virginia's heart continued to beat for the lost and outcast of the city. Sensing that God's plan for their lives involved continued full-time devotion to His work, Virginia and William applied to attend Mr. Moody's Chicago Bible Institute. In their student applications, they wrote that they wished to enroll in the urban evangelism program and wanted "to get a better knowledge of the Bible." The Bible Institute had grown, and in 1897, when the Ashers were accepted, it boasted four hundred students.

The one-year program at Moody's training school for Christian workers included a focus on Bible and theology. Christian service was an integral part of their Bible education, and Virginia found her place working alongside women like Sarah Dunn Clarke at the Pacific Garden Mission and Jessie Ackerman, of the Women's Christian Temperance Union (WCTU).[17] Fellow workers mentioned the "steady radiance" of Virginia's faith and her "devotion to duty in the midst of much physical fatigue and strain, her loyalty to Christ and to her fellow workers."[18]

Students from Moody's Bible Institute would use gospel wagons to take God's Word into the worst areas of the city where saloons, gambling, dance halls, and houses of prostitution lined the streets. These Christian women, who believed that God's Word was the solution to social problems, joined forces with organizations like the YWCA, the WCTU, and Social Purity to be

> *Virginia was beloved by "fallen women" and the madams who ran licensed houses of prostitution. She was often called in to read and pray with the sick, write letters to parents, dress wounds, and whisper words of peace to the dying.*

a "quiet, pervasive, personal influence" on society. They were convicted that by reaching women, they could have a positive effect on men.

Of special concern to Virginia were the women who were involved in prostitution. Unlike most religious men of his time, D. L. Moody felt that "women of ill repute" were victims. His sermon "The Prodigal Daughter" expressed an unusual sense of compassion for these women who were usually condemned and rejected by society. Moody wrote: "She is cast out and os-

tracized by society. She is condemned to an almost hopeless life of degradation and shame . . . but the wretch who has ruined her in body and soul holds his head high as ever and society attaches no stain to him."[19]

At the Pacific Garden Mission and other locations, Virginia would gather a number of "poor, unhappy girls" and plead with them to give their lives to Jesus. Many would break down in tears and accept Christ as well as help from

This woman, who was unable to have children of her own, "took in the world of lost souls and mothered them with Divine love."

the mission. Virginia had a warm and motherly manner that effectively broke through the resistance of even the most hardened souls and allowed them to finally realize God's love.

Mission meetings would often continue until the wee hours of the morning. Virginia's friend Helen Dixon wrote the two would often end up at the Federal Coffee Palace at four a.m., because it was open all night. "How delicious was the steaming cup of hot coffee which we enjoyed before turning in for a few hours rest before the soul-satisfying joy of another day's work for our blessed Lord," said Helen.[20]

Virginia and William's days were filled with Bible study and Christian work. They followed Moody's lead and sought out men and women in need—no matter how unsavory the location. One of their outreaches involved going into Chicago saloons, where only men were allowed. While not all saloons welcomed the intrusion of gospel workers, they would ask the bartender if they could put on a brief service for their patrons.

The Ashers and sometimes one additional friend would enter the saloon with a folding organ. Mrs. Asher would sing a familiar hymn. If the bartender was agreeable, he would introduce them to the customers and ask if they would stop drinking for a ten to twenty minute meeting. In some cases, the bartender would even cover the liquor bottles with long white cloths and insist that people quiet down for the service. "Such courtesy was amazing," wrote Helen, who often accompanied the Ashers. Virginia's singing always broke through hardened hearts, and William would follow with a message from God's Word.[21]

Following completion of their studies, William became assistant pastor of the Jefferson Park Presbyterian Church on the North Side of Chicago. Virginia was also asked to join their staff with a focus on women's work. But their time at the church would not be long. In 1900, they moved to Duluth, Minnesota, to supervise the Duluth's Bethel Rest rescue mission, an outreach for miners and lumbermen.[22] Virginia was known as the "mother" of that mission and again focused her work on reaching women who had fallen upon hard times. She worked with Duluth's prostitutes and their children. This woman, who was unable to have children of her own, "took in the world of lost souls and mothered them with divine love."[23]

Virginia's hair had begun to turn silver, and her figure had grown more "ample." At thirty-one, she no longer felt like a young girl. When she sang at services, her choice was often the hymn "My Mother's Prayer." As her voice sang the sentimental words, it evoked memories to all who listened of their mothers' prayers for them as children. It is said that many men would begin to "sob" as they remembered the teachings of their youth and considered turning back from their sinful ways.

William wrote a report back to their alma mater, Moody Bible Institute, in 1903, "We hold gospel meetings every evening. Seldom a night passes but what someone manifests a desire to lead a Christian life. God is prospering the work greatly, adding to Himself as wish to be saved."[24]

William told of one man, an alcoholic who had deserted his wife, who came to the mission and heard William speak about God and his responsibility. The wayward man decided to try to contact his wife, but at first received no response. Still concerned, he went in search of her and found her working as a servant in a wealthy home. She was not only destitute, but very ill. When he approached her, she began to cry and fell into his arms. "Oh Harry," she said.[25]

It was stories like this one, stories of healing and redemption, that kept William and Virginia focused on the difficult work reaching out to the lowest elements of society in the inner cities. They were a committed team who loved God and showed His love to each person, regardless of circumstance.

CHAPTER TWENTY

A Light for All Women

T he meeting hall was quiet. In the darkened room, Virginia Asher lit a single white tapered candle and held it high for all to see.

In the audience sat row after row of young women, each holding unlit candles. They came from shops and factories. They came from banks and offices. Some lived in difficult home situations. They looked at Virginia, the woman who had extended to them a hand of love and care, the woman who had challenged them to know God and His Word.

She was their beloved Torch Bearer. She had lit a flame in each of their lives and encouraged them to share God's love with others.

Virginia stepped off of the wooden platform and approached the first young girl. She touched the flame of her candle to the unlit wick and a new flame burst forth. One by one, the candles glowed and the girls began to sing. The women shed many tears as they felt the light of God sink deeply into their souls.

These meetings of the Virginia Asher Business Women's Council were the result of her faithful outreach to women. It was a work that began in the worst sections of Chicago and Duluth and continued until the end of her life.

After she and her husband left the Duluth rescue mission in 1905, they joined several traveling evangelistic campaigns—preaching and singing to hundreds of thousands across the country and the world.

The first campaign was led by an evangelist, Dr. J. Wilbur Chapman. The Ashers and others traveled with Chapman for seven years, holding revival meetings in cities across the country and eventually in eighteen countries. Her niece Edna remembered one Christmas, when Aunt "Ginny" and Uncle Will returned from an evangelistic trip to Egypt. Virginia would always bring back gifts for her nieces who she considered her "girls." This time, she surprised Edna and her sisters with dresses embroidered with King Tut designs. Between campaigns, Virginia and Will would return to Chicago and spend time with their families.[26]

On the road, the group would set up outreach meetings in prisons, seaports, churches, anywhere they could find a listening audience. For seven years, the group kept up the pace, moving from town to town.

Traveling for so many months and years was exhausting, and Virginia's health began to suffer. She stayed home for a bit to recuperate, and reestablished her long-lost friendship with Mr. and Mrs. Billy Sunday, whom she had met during her years in Chicago. Mr. Sunday had been saved through the outreach of the Pacific Garden Mission, where Virginia had volunteered, and now traveled himself as an evangelist.

It was during this period of their married life that William and Virginia were often separated by distance and ministry obligations. Though Virginia said they remained on friendly terms, they no doubt felt the loss of their earlier closeness. They were both doing what they loved, but no longer in the same place.

During one of Billy Sunday's meetings in Canton, Ohio, Mrs. Sunday was unable to accompany her husband, so Virginia was asked to go in her place. This was the beginning of a close partnership, where Virginia would lend her gift of song to Sunday's evangelistic meetings. Virginia traveled with the campaign for another seventeen years. She sang at each meeting, often singing duets with the well-known musician Homer Roderheaver. The two recorded many gospel albums together.[27]

Billy Sunday's purpose was simple—he wanted to bring the lost to Christ. He asked the members of his evangelistic party to pray for and seek out whatever group God was leading them to reach. Once again, Virginia showed her commitment to the working women, especially what she called the common shop and factory girl. In the early 1900s, women who worked outside of the home were considered "at risk" and vulnerable to temptation from their secular environment. Many of the women felt trapped in low-income work with little chance of improvement. Virginia's heart went out to these women. She wanted to offer them new purpose through Christ.

Mrs. Sunday admired Virginia's determination to reach these young women for the Lord. "She always did more than we could possibly expect her to do," said Mrs. Sunday. "She hath done what she could."[28] Virginia would arrange meetings that would fit the busy schedules of these women, at morning, noon, or another convenient time. Sometimes they would offer small luncheons or tea. The women came from stores, banks, factories, laundries, everywhere to hear this woman speak directly to them of God and His Word.

Virginia had an amazing memory for names. She would remember the name of each young woman—even those she had encountered months or years before.[29] It was her personal and emotional style that drew young women back to learn more.

Winnie Freeman wrote about a meeting at the Baptist Tabernacle in Atlanta, Georgia, where Virginia was scheduled to speak to women in the area. On a Sunday afternoon, five hundred women gathered to hear Virginia Asher. "The auditorium was filled, every seat taken, and along the edges of the rooms women were lined several deep, standing."[30]

Virginia was not a typical preacher. Winnie said that she wore a plum-colored satin dress, had wavy silver hair and a mellow voice. With love in her eyes, Virginia told the women the story of another woman who approached Jesus in the home of a man named Simon. This woman had washed the Lord's feet with her tears, anointing Him with perfume. When Virginia finished speaking, Winnie notes that "hundreds in the audience were weeping."

Virginia addressed the women, "I am asking you this afternoon if you are willing to lay aside the things that have taken so much of your time that you haven't had time for Christ. Are you willing to lay your all upon the altar?"[31]

Women responded well to these meetings, perhaps because they were so unusual in that male-centered society. While there were women of all ages in attendance, men were strangely absent in the crowd. The only man present was the occasional janitor. There were women serving as ushers, women passing the offering plates, and women leading the prayer and singing. Virginia urged this community of women to read their Bibles and to let the words of Scripture affect their lives.[32]

She also established a mentoring relationship between women who were "professionals"—nurses, teachers, etc., and the "common" workers. She felt that by introducing these friendships, women would help one another, both in business and in their personal faith.

As a result of these meetings that had begun on the Billy Sunday campaign trail, a national network of women's groups was formed. While Virginia wasn't particularly concerned about building a formal organization, the women wanted a way to ensure that the work would continue in the cities where the evangelistic campaigns had traveled. The groups were first simply called Bible classes, but eventually grew into the Virginia Asher Business Women's Council.

In the 1920s, Virginia and William moved to Winona Lake, Indiana, to a lovely roomy cottage where they could adapt a more restful pace and be near to their good friends, the Sundays. They were also able to finally be together in one place. Virginia enjoyed a bit more leisure here and was able to enjoy the occasional game of golf or croquet. She loved poetry, her favorite poet being Tennyson.[33] But despite this break from travel, Virginia's work with women intensified.

It was here that a more formal committee began, in 1922, to organize the council. Their purpose was "to promote a spirit of friendliness, helpfulness, and responsibility for other girls among all business women of the city and to associate them in personal loyalty to Jesus Christ."[34]

The women were given Bibles and encouraged to read some each day and to memorize Scripture. One bookstore owner promised a free Scofield Bible to any woman who could memorize and recite five hundred Bible verses with their references.[35]

The association encouraged the women to think about missions—the work of the gospel across the nation and the world. One of the group's projects grew out of a talk by a Dr. Biederwolf in 1923. Visiting the Business Council, he talked about the need for the care of lepers in Korea. The council members were intrigued and wanted to hear more. How could they help?

In 1925, the conference voted to raise funds to build a hospital in connection with the doctor's work with lepers in Korea. It was named in honor of the founder, The Virginia Asher Hospital for Lepers in Soonchun. Another work involved the support of displaced Jews in Poland.[36]

Soon after, they heard from a woman who worked in the mountains of Virginia. She told of the need at the Cumberland Mountain Mission. The women, eager to help, gathered boxes of clothing and sent money to this, their first home missions project.[37]

As the work grew, Virginia Asher continued to be a very involved leader. She would travel to visit the councils in Kentucky, Tennessee, and Virginia.

"There is reason for their devotion to her," wrote one friend, "for love shines in her every look and word. She has never adopted the attitude of a dictator, but that of a kindly advisor."[38]

At the council meetings, Virginia loved to use creative and dramatic ways to illustrate God's love to the women and to engage their emotions. Her niece told of one time when she spoke to the women while standing on a boat on a small Indiana lake. Her theme song was "The Light of the World Is Jesus." At the end of the meeting, she would begin to sing the song and the girls would join in. Then, as their voices rose, the boat would be propelled slowly across the water and Virginia's voice would trail softly across to the shore.[39] Her messages were haunting and inspirational.

Women loved their Torch Bearer and prayed for her on a regular basis—some say that not a day went by that a woman somewhere did not utter a prayer for Virginia Asher.[40] During her later years, Virginia struggled with her health. It was William who cared for her during those years, the two drawn back together after years of traveling apart.

Virginia died, at age sixty-eight, in February of 1937; William would soon follow to their heavenly home in November. But despite her eternal home going, the Torch Bearer had lit a flame that continued to burn. At one of her memorial services, held at councils across the country, one member wrote in tribute:

> A torch she is holding; she goes on before—
> "Girls, study the Word; glean the truth o'er and o'er;
> Then go as it bids you; seek others each day,
> Bring them to the Savior, the Life, Truth and Way."[41]

FANNY CROSBY

1820–1915

Fanny Crosby, holding her signature book. (Moody Bible Institute Crowell Library archives)

Fanny Crosby in her later years. (Moody Bible Institute Crowell Library archives)

Fanny Crosby loved speaking to children.
(Moody Bible Institute Crowell Library archives)

Fanny and one of her favorite
co-composers, Ira Sankey. (Moody
Bible Institute Crowell Library
archives)

"EMMA" EMELINE E. DRYER

1835–1925

Emma Dryer as a young woman. (Moody Bible Institute Crowell Library archives)

Evangelist Dwight L. Moody, at the time of the founding of the Chicago school. (Moody Bible Institute Crowell Library archives)

Emma's portrait as the head of the Chicago Bible Institute—an oil painting of this photo hangs in the Moody Historical Museum at Moody Bible Institute. (Moody Bible Institute Crowell Library archives)

The Chicago campus of Moody Bible Institute as it appears today. (Moody Bible Institute Crowell Library archives)

"NETTIE" NANCY (FOWLER) McCORMICK

1835–1923

Portrait of Nettie Fowler McCormick 1862. (Courtesy of the Wisconsin Historical Society)

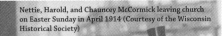

Cyrus Hall McCormick and his wife, Nettie, in Chicago, Illinois. 1884. (Courtesy of the Wisconsin Historical Society).

Nettie, Harold, and Chauncey McCormick leaving church on Easter Sunday in April 1914 (Courtesy of the Wisconsin Historical Society)

SARAH DUNN CLARKE

1835–1918

A gathering of Pacific Garden Mission workers and friends for a picnic. In the center of the photo is Sarah Dunn Clarke and (just to her left in the darker blouse) her friend, Nettie McCormick. (Courtesy of the Pacific Garden Mission)

The chapel at the Pacific Garden Mission in its beginning years. (Courtesy of the Pacific Garden Mission)

Sarah Dunn Clarke (Courtesy of the Pacific Garden Mission)

An early photo of the Pacific Garden Mission office, with Sarah's portrait on the wall. (Courtesy of the Pacific Garden Mission)

AMANDA SMITH

1837–1915

Amanda Berry Smith in her signature Quaker style outfit (courtesy of Moody Bible Institute, Crowell Library Archives).

Amanda's daughter, Mazie.

Amanda's adopted son, Bob.

VIRGINIA ASHER

1869–1937

Miss Saxe — "Rody" — Miss Sunday.

B.D. Ackley. W.A.Sunday Miss Miller.

1915 Mrs. Asher. The Sunday Party

Billy Sunday and his team of evangelists, including Virginia Asher (with glasses) and her husband William, second from left. (Courtesy of Billy Graham Center Archives)

Billy Sunday and team of evangelists, including Virginia. (Courtesy of Billy Graham Center Archives)

THE SUNDAY PARTY

EVANGELINE BOOTH

1865–1950

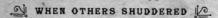

A young Evangeline Booth in Salvation Army garb. (Courtesy of the Salvation Army)

Evangeline Booth administrating the Salvation Army in the United States. (Courtesy of the Salvation Army)

Evangeline Booth addressing her colleagues as their Commander. (Courtesy of the Salvation Army)

MARY MCLEOD BETHUNE

1875–1955

Mary McLeod Bethune and some of her first students in Daytona, Florida. (Courtesy of Florida Memory Project)

Mary McLeod Bethune and her classmates at Moody Bible Institute (Courtesy of the Moody Bible Institute Crowell Library Archives)

Mary McLeod Bethune walking up the steps of the White House on an official visit. (Courtesy of the Florida Memory Project)

Bethune-Cookman University in Daytona Beach, Florida, today.

EVANGELINE BOOTH

BOOTH

1865–1950

CHAPTER TWENTY-ONE

Called to Serve

—••— ❧⸱❧ —••—

Eva adjusted the dark, wide-brimmed, fabric bonnet on her head, tucking in the last strands of her unruly, wavy, dark brown hair. Her mother, Catherine, tied the oversized satin bow just a bit off-center underneath her chin.

At age fifteen, in the year 1880, Eva Booth was being commissioned as a sergeant in the Salvation Army.

In a burst of excitement, the young girl threw her arms around her mother, the joy and honor of the moment overwhelming her. She knew that "sergeant" was the lowest rank in their volunteer "army," and that suited her just fine. Since her parents were the founders of the organization, she didn't want anyone to accuse them of favoritism.

Her parents were proud of their daughter. Catherine looked into Eva's eyes—she seemed so grown-up in the official "army" uniform—and gave her a kiss. Now Eva was not just her physical daughter, but they were sisters in a common cause, reaching the world for God.

Evelyne Cory Booth was born on Christmas morning in 1865. She was the daughter of Catherine and William Booth, the seventh of their eight children.[1] Her parents were deeply religious and socially conscious of the troubles facing the lower class citizens of England. Her mother wanted to name her "Eva" after one of the characters in the novel *Uncle Tom's Cabin*, but her father insisted on the more formal "Evelyne." Despite the name on her birth certificate, she was then known as "Eva."

The same year of Eva's birth, William and Catherine began an organization of Christian volunteers to help the poor and evangelize the lost in urban England. Searching for a name to call the group, they thought of "Volunteer Army"—but felt it lacking. Instead, their church became known as the Salvation Army, and members embodied a military style in their uniforms, flag, and rankings. William focused on preaching to the down and out of society, while Catherine approached the wealthy for financial support. Together, they believed in the three "S"s while reaching those who the rest of society rejected: first, soup; second, soap; and third, salvation.[2]

The Booths wanted to pass on their faith to their children, and the Bible was a common theme in their home. In the nursery was a huge Noah's Ark complete with wooden animals. The ark was reserved as a plaything to be used only on Sundays. The rest of the days, the animals would be neatly lined up waiting for the ark to open its great doors. In a burst of authenticity, the children would sometimes choose one of the animals to "sacrifice" and a little charcoal circle was embedded on the play table.[3]

Eva loved to write stories and act in plays. After debating whether or not music was too frivolous a pursuit, the Booths purchased a piano and Eva tried her hand at writing hymns. The house was full of joy and song as well as biblical discipline. Eva loved animals, especially her dog named Nelson. After Nelson died, she became especially fond of a monkey that she named Little Jeannie. The precocious animal was known to love women's finery and, much to her parents' dismay, would leap onto the heads of unsuspecting female visitors.

One day, Eva made a miniature Salvation Army uniform for Little Jeannie. Her mom, upon seeing the fully dressed pet, shook her head with a smile and told Eva to take it off. "Why?" asked Eva. "Because," explained her mom, "he isn't living the life. A man can be changed, but once a monkey, always a monkey."[4]

One biographer described Eva as "a slender slip of a thing with a very decided will of her own, observant, missing nothing."[5] She was athletic and brave. She had not been raised a serene, proper Christian, but one who was determined to make a historic difference in the world.

At ten years old, her mother took her to an art museum where she remembers seeing the painting *Christ Standing Before Pilate*. Young Eva stood motionless, staring at the painting. Finally, she burst into tears. "Will no one come out to help Him?" she asked. "Why does not some strong man shoot them down?"[6]

This serious nature led to her following directly in her parents' footsteps and desiring to join the Lord's Army as a full-fledged member. She was commissioned and fitted with the uniform and bonnet. The bonnet the women wore as a part of their uniform had been designed by the Puritans and Quakers, who continued to wear it long after it had gone out of fashion. For them, and for the Salvation Army officers, it was a visible symbol of their faith and service.

Spreading their faith in London was certainly a battle. Eva began participating in her parents' ministry by selling *War Cry*—the news bulletin of the Salvation Army. This involved her going into very poor and sometimes unsafe neighborhoods. While the Salvation Army won the hearts and respect of some, they also angered others, because of their outspoken opinions against the use and sale of alcohol.

From those involved in the liquor trade, a group rose up, naming themselves the Skeleton Army. Their main purpose was to harass members of the Salvation Army. They would throw bones, rocks, rats, and tar at the Army members, causing riots to break out on the streets. In one incident, they grabbed at the ribbons of Eva's uniform, and a missile struck her forehead, causing it to bleed. The Army workers had hot water dumped on them from windows above, in addition to curses by onlookers.[7] Despite the conflicts, Evelyne refused to give up her cause or allow anyone to intimidate her.

When she realized the gap separating her from the people at the base of society, she decided to cross those boundaries creatively. She dressed herself in a ragged outfit and mingled with other flower girls beside the fountain at Piccadilly Circus in the slums.[8] Upon returning to her home after a night on the cold streets, she wrote, "Men, women, and children with broken lives, broken hearts and broken character: hopeless and help-less, trapped like animals at bay."[9]

One particular girl broke her heart, a fifteen-year-old mother with despair in her "frightened blue eyes." The girl told Evelyne, "There is no place for us in life or death; no place for the baby or for me."

Brokenhearted, Evelyne composed a hymn called "The Wounds of Christ": "The wounds of Christ are open, Sinner they were made for thee; The wounds of Christ are open. There for refuge flee." During those years, she made a name for herself as the "White Angel of the Slums."[10]

In her first years with the Salvation Army, Eva had grown into a confident and gifted speaker. One biographer noted, "So absorbed were her audiences in her sincerity that she was able to stand silent before thousands for a minute at a time amid a profound still-ness. 'If anyone had coughed,' said one listener, 'I should have fainted.'"[11]

> "So absorbed were her audiences in her sincerity that she was able to stand silent before thousands for a minute at a time amid a profound stillness. 'If anyone had coughed,' said one listener, 'I should have fainted.'"

While she was now a young woman, she was also still her mother's daughter. In 1886, her mother wrote a letter to her daughter, urging her to take care of herself and to be encouraged. "My dearest Eva, Your letter has been long in coming, but I was very glad to get it. . . . I cannot understand about you being so down. What is it about? Face the question for yourself and look at your mercies. You are only twenty. Your health is improving. You have already such a position as many, even public women, don't reach in half a lifetime. You have the love and care of parents and brothers and sisters such as few have. You have the chance if you will use it of improving yourself as much as you like, and you have such an object in life as no other girl in the world has! Now why with so much should you be so down?"

Her mother writes with advice and encouragement to her daughter, "Don't allow [yourself to think that yours are] imaginary but rise up in the strength of God and resolve to conquer. Do."[12]

And Eva did. Whenever there were problems in an outlying ministry of the Army's activities, William Booth was known to say, "Send Eva!" She became increasingly involved in every part of her father's work. She became acquainted with great men and women of the faith including evangelist Dwight L. Moody, who was a good friend to her father, and Frances Willard, founder of the Women's Christian Temperance Union.

Willard was known, not just for her efforts on behalf of women's suffrage and temperance, but also on protecting the rights of underprivileged women and children. It was Willard who suggested that Eva change her name to "Evangeline" because it was more dignified and reflected her desire to give her life as an evangelist.[13]

Just two years later, when Eva was twenty-three, her mother was diagnosed with breast cancer. Catherine's case was considered incurable, and she was given only two years to live. Eva's father was inconsolable at the prospect of losing his beloved wife and ministry partner. The next year, as he turned sixty, friends gave a birthday banquet in his honor. Catherine was unable to sit at the dinner, so she lay in a nearby bed, frail but cheerful.

That next year, when Catherine realized the end of her life's journey was near, she took off her wedding ring and slipped it onto her husband's finger. She told him, "By this token we were united for time and by it we are now united for eternity."[14]

To Eva, she turned and holding her daughter close, whispered, "My Christmas Box! Don't fret. You'll follow me! I'll watch for you."[15] For eighteen years, William wore his wife's ring. When he died, he sent the ring to Eva—telling her it was on her mother's finger the Christmas morning she was born.

Despite her sorrow, Eva honored her mother's memory by pushing forward with her work. In the next years, William would send two of his daughters to America and Canada—to supervise the Army's work on foreign soil.

For both Eva and Emma, their voyage to America would be life changing.

CHAPTER TWENTY-TWO

San Francisco and Soapy Smith

❧ ──── ⚬⚬ ❦ ⚬⚬ ──── ❧

When Evangeline arrived in San Francisco, just one month after the great earthquake and fire, the charred remains and physical needs of the city's thousands of homeless were overwhelming.

On April 18, 1906, in the early hours of the morning, a massive earthquake had traumatized the region surrounding the city of San Francisco. Residents were awakened to violent shaking of their homes. The quake ripped apart roads, tore off the fronts of buildings, and damaged the city's water mains. Immediately afterward, a fire began that roared through the city, consuming everything in its wake for two days. Due to the lack of water supply, the blaze went completely unchecked.

Still recovering from shock, residents frantically left their homes, dragging trunks and suitcases crammed with their possessions. One elderly woman refused to leave her home until two policemen picked her up and carried her to a waiting horse and wagon.[16] Most of the city was destroyed. There were no street lights and no lights in most of the homes. Everything was dark. Many streets were impassable because walls had collapsed and rubble covered every inch of the ground. Most stores and factories were burned down, leaving people without food and jobs. The city was filled with smoldering ash.[17]

Included in the more than 2,500 acres and 28,000 buildings destroyed by the fire, was the local headquarters of the Salvation Army. All of their equipment was gone. Refusing to despair, the volunteers quickly set up a rescue camp for the thousands of refugees fleeing the city. Workers quickly sent for supplies and distributed clothing, food, and water. A reporter from the *San Francisco Examiner* interviewed one Salvation Army volunteer who said, "We are always ready for an emergency." Their brave, quick-thinking response backed up that bold statement.[18]

Evangeline later wrote about the earthquake, "The majority of the people who escaped had nothing but their nightclothes—the earthquake taking place at four in the morning. Something like forty babies were born the first day after the disaster, nearly all of them on the bare ground."[19]

Back in New York, U. S. Commander Evangeline Booth set about raising funds to support the rescue efforts in San Francisco. She held a meeting in New York's Union Square where she collected twelve thousand dollars. Workers collected additional pennies, nickels, and dimes in Christmas kettles carried throughout the crowd.[20]

In May, Evangeline traveled to see the disaster for herself. She rode eight thousand miles in twelve days to view the area. Up until that point, the Salvation Army had kept its relief work quiet, because they did not have the financial means to serve as an official disaster agency. But in this instance, they proved themselves necessary and capable of rising to such an occasion.[21]

In the sixteen years following her mother's death, Evangeline's life had been filled with changes, both good and bad. An attractive, athletic woman standing five feet, ten inches, she had many proposals of marriage. But Evangeline had decided that she would remain single. In discussions with her father, they agreed that the independent life not only suited her best, but would allow her to pursue her goals without being weighed down by the demands of a house and family.

At age thirty-three, at her father's bidding, she traveled to Canada and Alaska where she supervised the Salvation Army's work among the settlers and prospectors heading west in search of riches during the Klondike Gold Rush. Tales were told about a time she came face-to-face with a notorious outlaw named Soapy Smith. Smith had earned his name selling bars of soap. He told customers that some bars of soap were wrapped with money, and they might win a great fortune. Of course, the only bars with money were given to members of his own gang—it was merely a con.

Soapy Smith was a tall, scowling man, who owned a local saloon and was notorious for criminal activity. His gang of about sixty men terrorized every town they visited. According to legend, when Smith decided to attend a Salvationist meeting, Evangeline told her coworkers, "Leave him to me." She offered the man a cup of cocoa and asked him, "Why don't you give up this kind of life?"

Smith told Evangeline that if he surrendered to police, he would be put to death. Agreed, said Evangeline, but salvation offers victory over death. The outlaw listened to Evangeline's prayer and then departed, soon to die in a gun fight. She would never know if their brief interaction had softened the criminal's heart.[22]

While Evangeline served the Salvation Army up north, her sister, Emma, was working with her husband in the United States. Both were successful in their work, far exceeding their father's expectations. Evangeline's records indicated that the summer of 1902 included ninety meetings held by the Salvation Army in Canada with more than thirty thousand attending and 350 making commitments to Christ.[23]

One day, Emma sent word that Evangeline would soon become an aunt—and they had decided to name the little one "Evangeline," in her honor. This made what happened next even more painful. Shortly after birth, her newborn niece died, and Evangeline traveled to New York, heartbroken, to conduct the memorial service for the tiny girl and her bereaved parents.

Then, in 1903, the Booths faced yet another tragedy. Emma had been killed in a train derailment, her head dealt a fatal blow when the passenger car left the tracks. The Booths were in shock, although they firmly believed that death for a believer was merely a "promotion to glory." Once again, Evangeline traveled to New York City where a service was held in Carnegie Hall. Nearly 75,000 mourners came to pay their respects to the family who had given their lives to serve the needs of so many.[24]

Emma's death, while it dealt an emotional blow, also prompted a new role for Evangeline in the Salvation Army. In 1904, she was appointed to head up the efforts in the United States. For the next thirty years, she would serve as the Commander of the Salvation Army's United States operation, headquartered in New York City.[25]

Evangeline helped to firmly establish the Salvation Army in the United States, reaching thousands of people with God's message and raising millions of dollars for the cause.[26] At that time, her father was seventy-five years old, and her brother Bramwell had been appointed his chief of staff. The Salvation Army continued to be a family concern. Her dad would also send messages of support to his daughter. He urged her to use funds to buy a basic automobile to get from place to place—not wanting to have his daughter be a "strap hanger" on street cars any longer.

When she was forty-one, she helped the Salvation Army respond to its first major natural catastrophe in the United States, the earthquake in San

Francisco. Her bold actions and ability to draw the crowds with stirring words raised funds for the relief work and established the Salvation Army as a forceful presence in the United States and around the world.

Six years later, in 1912, her father, William Booth, was "promoted to glory." William Booth knew that the future of the organization that he and Catherine had devoted their lives to was in good hands with their children. Evangeline was not able to be at her father's bedside, but sent a cable saying, "Kiss him for me."[27]

It was reported that millions of people crowded London streets to honor the man who had done so much on behalf of their country. The closest comparison for us today would be the crowds that gathered to honor Princess Diana in 1997; Booth's procession drew crowds double that size.[28]

In response, King George V wrote to Bramwell Booth about his father, William, "The nation has lost a great organizer and the poor a whole-hearted and sincere friend, who devoted his life to helping them in a practical way." One biographer wrote that forty thousand people attended the funeral service and among the crowd were "thieves, tramps, harlots, the lost and outcast to whom Booth had given his heart." Unnoticed at the back sat Queen Mary, wife of King George V.[29]

The Booth family mourned, but Evangeline was not dismayed. While her mother, father, and sister had preceded her to heaven, she had plenty of work to do on earth. She was called to reach the world for God.

CHAPTER TWENTY-THREE

The World for God

I t is not how many years we live, but rather what we do with them," said Evangeline Cory Booth.[30]

It was not long after Evangeline's father, William, died that war broke out in Europe. For years, they had heard rumblings of threats. Then, in 1917, the United States entered the war and sent thousands of America's brave young men to the front lines.

As the head of the operations of the Salvation Army in the United States, Evangeline Booth was dedicated to serving the needs of the military. She sent volunteers to Europe to do what they could: providing canteens in dugouts, free refreshments, religious services, musical concerts, and even mending clothes.

In a controversial move, Evangeline also decided to send 250 Salvation Army women officers to the war front in France. Before they left, she prayed with them, asking God's blessings and divine protection. She gave them copies of the Salvation Army newspaper *War Cry* in French, to distribute to the people.

One of the girls, assigned to the American First Division, decided to fry some dough as a treat for the soldiers. The young woman later wrote, "There was also a prayer in my heart that somehow this home touch would do more for those who ate the doughnuts than satisfy a physical hunger." The women soon became known as "Doughnut Girls," distributing from

2,500 to 9,000 doughnuts each day to the men who stood in line with their feet in the rain and mud waiting for the treats.[31]

Evangeline's life was busy and fulfilling, and she often thought very little of her own personal comfort and needs. In Canada she had purchased a house for an extremely low price because it was rumored to be haunted. As she did the work of the Salvation Army in New York, she again bought a property for a bargain sum because it was next to a dog's cemetery.[32] Although she would never marry and bear children of her own, Evangeline eventually adopted four children, reflecting her tender affection for little ones, especially those in need.

During her first Christmas in New York, she was overwhelmed by the tremendous poverty that surrounded her, especially among children. She estimated that nearly seventy thousand children were in need of food and were going without breakfast. She had the Salvation Army organize breakfast lines and her volunteers delivered baskets of food that families could enjoy in the privacy of their own homes.[33]

The work of the Salvation Army quickly expanded—and under her leadership their properties and financing grew. During her thirty years as leader, she increased their stations of operation from 696 to 1600.[34] She was called upon to make fair judgments regarding issues large and small, such as, "Should a girl in the Army be allowed to cut her front hair into a 'bang'?" and "What about a design for a hot weather uniform?"[35] She was decisive and, through the years, proved a fair, energetic, and capable leader.

Evangeline Booth became renowned throughout the United States for her work with the Salvation Army. In 1930, she was asked to visit President Franklin D. Roosevelt at the White House, and, in 1932, she gave the invocation at the Chicago Democratic Convention. Her competent work did not go unnoticed.

In 1934, when Evangeline was sixty-nine, the Salvation Army made a momentous decision and named her as the first woman to lead the international efforts of the Salvation Army as its General. President Roosevelt sent his official congratulations at her official inauguration ceremony, "In these troubled times, it is particularly important that the leadership of all good forces shall be for the amelioration of human suffering and for the preservation of the highest spiritual ideals. Through your efforts as Commander in Chief you have earned the gratitude and admiration of millions of your countrymen. I am confident that under your guidance the Salvation Army will go steadily forward in service to the unfortunate of every land."[36]

While she had been promoted to a position of great responsibility, supervising the worldwide operation of the Salvation Army, she never lost her ability to touch individual people. She remained dedicated, especially to the needs of children. She started an orphanage in Liverpool named Strawberry Field—a home that would later inspire John Lennon to write a song for The Beatles.

She told one reporter, "Last night at dusk, I was walking briskly up and down the lovely road in front of my home when two little colored children approached me. The braver of the two said timidly, 'How do you do?' I replied, 'How do YOU do?' She then looked up at me and said, 'Are you the lady as what is always doing something for somebody?' I was touched because it seemed to me that the baby, with her one phrase, had exactly described the Salvation Army's work."[37]

As the fourth general of the Salvation Army, Evangeline toured the world, to see the work of the Salvation Army in India, Australia, New Zealand, Germany, and England. Shaking hands and being greeted in a multitude of languages, she was awed to see the people of God serving Him in so many lands, in so many ways, to so many people whose lives had benefited from the Army's efforts.

Although she was given many awards and honorary degrees, for Evangeline life was never about herself and only about the work at hand. Even as she neared the age that many would retire, she refused to rest. In 1937, as the world faced a second war, she personally escorted fifteen hundred of London's poorest children for a day in the country. She provided meals for the children, gave them rides on a merry-go-round, and greeted them with an encouraging message, finally leading them in a song.

At seventy-two, she was as involved in the ministry and with the people she served as the day she first tied the ribbon on her bonnet at age fifteen.

Her beliefs were expressed in her speeches, books, and hymns. In her book, *Toward a Better World*, she wrote:

> *The world is ever repeating the inquiry, "What is religion"? I have the answer: Religion is a life in harmony with the will of God. It permeates everything; it is of no value unless it molds and governs every circumstance of life. Neither Earth nor Heaven has any use for religion that is like a best jacket—hung on the back on the Sabbath, and hung in the cupboard through the week.* [38]

In England, during the coronation of Edward, Prince of Wales, she was honored as a special guest. Princesses Elizabeth and Margaret sang the chorus of her song "The World for God." The words of that hymn, penned in 1934, beautifully reflected her life's mission. She had written the lyrics when she was awakened at three o'clock in the morning, aware of the "stupendous responsibilities of the call that had come to me on being elected General of the International Salvation Army."

> *The world for God! The world for God!*
> *There's nothing else will meet the hunger of my soul.*
> *I see forsaken children. I see the tears that fall.*
> *From women's eyes once merry, now never laugh at all;*
> *I see the sins and sorrows of those who sit in darkness;*
> *I see in lands far distant, the hungry and oppressed.*
> *The world for God! The world for God!*
> *I give my heart! I'll do my part! The world for God.* [39]

Evangeline Booth's term as General ended in 1939. When she turned seventy-four, she returned to America to retire to Acadia, the home she had built years earlier. It was difficult for this woman, whose entire life had been spent in active service, to slow down. Never one to rest, she would mount her horse, Golden Heart, in the mornings and enjoy a quiet ride.

Evangeline Booth died in her home on July 17, 1950, at the age of eighty-four from arteriosclerosis. Although she was "promoted to glory," she left a rich legacy. Today, the Salvation Army continues to serve the world for Christ, working in ninety-one different countries meeting the needs of the poor and the spiritually lost.

CHAPTER TWENTY-FOUR

Women and Politics

———⟶⟳⟵———

On August 6, 1920, American women were granted the right to vote. But their involvement in politics had begun with a vengeance more than fifty years earlier.

In 1851, abolitionist and ex-slave Sojourner Truth stood and spoke out for equality in Ohio. She gave her famous speech "Ain't I a Woman" that left a lasting impact on her audience. Although the cause was gaining momentum, the fight for a woman's right to vote was set aside during the Civil War as everyone's attention turned to what most felt was the much more pressing issue of abolishing slavery.

In the mid-1850s, the women's voice grew as they spoke and acted out against issues that concerned them. In December of 1873, women in Ohio, New York, and other states shut down several thousand saloons in a protest against the evils of alcohol consumption.[1]

In 1874, the Women's Christian Temperance Union (WCTU) was formed led by Frances Willard. The WCTU blamed alcohol for societal problems like domestic violence and abuse. These women had seen men squander their family's savings in saloons.

Frances Willard believed that the only way to really change the law would be for women to gain the right to vote. Her political concerns extended beyond alcohol to include the need for public education, free lunches for children, unions for workers, and limits to the workday. They

fought the evils of prostitution and introduced legislation that would protect women and children from rape and abuse. Willard argued to raise the
age of sexual consent for females from the current law of seven or ten years
of age, to the age of sixteen.[2]

The WCTU, led completely by women, became a powerful organization.
They worked to influence government and society as well as spread the
gospel. Willard said of her "army" of committed women: "These make an
aggregate of several thousands of women who are regularly studying and
expounding God's word to the multitude . . ."[3]

For these women, politics and their Christian faith were closely inter-
twined. The WCTU provided many Christian women with their first opportunities to be involved in organizational activity and public speaking.
Amanda Berry Smith, Fanny Crosby, and Evangeline Booth were all speakers on behalf of the organization.

The growth of the WCTU was a huge help as women fought for their
right to vote. For years, they had argued that they should have the right to
vote because they were created equal. Now, they added that women should
be allowed to vote because they were *different* than men. Women, they said,
could help create a more pure, moral, and gentle society. The fight was long
and hard. Women would wait until 1920 to win the right to cast their vote.

Women's clubs were popular at the turn of the century as a way for
women to work together to better society. These social clubs were prevalent
among both white and black women. In Chicago around this time, African-
American women were involved in more than 150 such clubs. While some
of these groups were purely social, most of them worked toward societal
and political reform. They helped establish kindergartens and fought for
anti-lynching laws. They were involved in suffrage, temperance, and raising money for charitable organizations. In her book *Toward a Tenderer Humanity and a Nobler Womanhood*, Anne Meis Knupfer describes the role of

these clubs. Their motivation often came from their "deep-seated Christian faith."[4]

Christian women were often sought after by government leaders to speak to important issues. When Mary McLeod Bethune was invited to the White House by President Franklin D. Roosevelt to help address the problems of "her people," she became an outspoken advocate for the rights of the American Negro in her day.

When Christian women became involved in facing the problems of their society, they were often drawn into the realm of politics. They felt compelled to speak up against evil. They actively supported charitable organizations. They bonded together to influence their world for good. These women saw involvement in politics as a necessary way to better the world for God's glory.

MARY MCLEOD BETHUNE

1875–1955

CHAPTER TWENTY-FIVE

Longing to Learn

Mary Jane McLeod quickly pulled back her hand and winced—the dried bristle of the cotton plant had left a long, red stinging cut across her skin. Sighing, she picked up a corner of her apron to wipe the cut clean. The day was steamy, and the sun unrelenting. Since four a.m., long before the sun came up, she had been picking cotton in the fields with her parents, brothers, and sisters.

She was a hard worker—fast, steady, and determined. While the other kids sometimes snuck off to rest or play in the shade, Mary Jane refused to quit. Her picking record thus far was 250 pounds of cotton in one day.

Mary Jane was born July 10, 1875, in Mayesville, South Carolina, to former slaves Samuel and Patsy McLeod. Mary Jane was the fifteenth of seventeen children and the first child born after President Abraham Lincoln's Emancipation Proclamation had declared them free. After continuing to work for the slave owners for a few years to save money, the McLeods were finally able to purchase a small plot of land to farm on their own. Mary Jane remembers how they fought to clear the land from crabgrass with their old family mule named "Old Bush" for his bushy tale. When the mule finally dropped dead, the family took turns pulling the plow over the hard soil.[1]

Life was not easy, but the McLeod family knew how to work hard and they loved one another through each step of their journey, no matter how difficult. Her parents realized that, of all their children, Mary Jane was different. She was homely, but bright.

Her mother said, "Mary Jane has a rising soul. She will either go far or break her heart."[2] Mary Jane recognized that God alone could help them. Each night she would pray to God that she could be educated—and, most of all, to be delivered from the crabgrass! Her parents cherished their new-found freedom and repeated stories of when and how they had heard the great announcement.

Booker T. Washington remembered being only nine years old when the freeing of the slaves was announced:

> As the great day drew nearer, there was more singing in the slave quarters than usual. It was bolder, had more ring, and lasted later into the night. After the reading [of the Proclamation] we were told that we were all free, and could go when and where we pleased. My mother, who was standing by my side, leaned over and kissed her children, while tears of joy ran down her cheeks. She explained to us what it all meant, that this was the day for which she had been so long praying, but fearing that she would never live to see.[3]

"Free," Mary Jane loved the sound of that word. It meant that no one could own her or her family or her people, that she was her own person. She could be who she wanted to be—anything in the world.

Mary Jane had a few secret wishes. First, she wanted to have glass windows in her house. In their small wooden cabin, the windows were closed with wooden boards. She had seen the houses of white people when she went with her parents to work. They had clear glass that allowed light to come streaming in. How wonderful it would be to sit by such a window and gaze out at the world.

She had another wish as well. She wanted to learn to read. The white children, in their homes with glass windows, had shelves filled with books.

She couldn't read them—no one in her family could. She wanted to learn to read—she wanted, more than anything else, to get an education.

As an adult, Mary remembered the deep longing in her heart for something more, "When I was a little child kneeling under the old apple tree in the corner of our garden. My hands were clasped and my eyes turned heavenward. Oh how fervently I besought the great Spirit which I could not see, but felt, to open the way for me to become trained and prepared so that I might leave the cotton field and go out into the great world and do a great work of service."[4]

One day, a local missionary approached the family and asked if they could spare one child to attend her school. Mary Jane's mom, recognizing that her daughter was different from the rest of her children, chose her to attend. It was a long walk for the young girl, five miles. It was a humble one-room school with painted cardboard for a blackboard, but Mary Jane was thrilled. She was learning to read and to do sums.

She could help her family figure the weight of cotton picked by each person—and what each should be paid.[5] She gathered the other children and taught them how to read as well. The teacher gave Mary Jane a Bible and let her read John 3:16. The Bible said "whosoever," noticed Mary Jane. "It didn't say black or white—it just said 'whosoever.'"

When she had finished her education at the local school, the family needed her to return to the fields. High school was not available for Negro children in her area. She wondered if she might live the rest of her years walking behind a plow. As she trudged through the field, she asked the Lord to provide a way. "God did not forget me," said Mary.[6]

A missionary woman came with news. Mary Chrissman, a Quaker from Denver, Colorado, had given a scholarship that would allow one Negro girl to attend the Scotia Seminary in Concord, North Carolina.

Mary, hearing the news, pulled the cotton sack from her shoulder, fell on her knees, and turned her eyes heavenward, thanking God. This had to be the answer to her silent prayers. Tearfully, her mother packed a small sack of her belongings. Her father, not usually given to emotion, hugged his young daughter close. They were sad, but also rejoicing. This was what they had often dreamed of—that God would send them signs of hope and a brighter future for their children. Mary would lead the way.

"Whenever the Lord says no to me," said Mary, *"I look into my heart and search my motives. For it is only the selfless me that God can use."*

Mary took a train ride, her first, to North Carolina. Stepping out of the carriage, she saw the school building, made of red brick and containing glass windows. The new world seemed brighter than she had even imagined. At that school she learned about Christian teachings of equality for all people. She also felt a calling from God for missionary service. She felt a deep longing to travel the world and began to desire to serve God as a missionary to Africa.

At Scotia Seminary, Mary worked in the laundry to help support her education. She was acclaimed the best laundress in the school, and the president would request that she be the one to launder his shirts.[7] Whatever Mary was asked to do, she did it with excellence and a positive spirit.

When she finished her education at Scotia Seminary, her donor, Miss Chrissman, said she wanted to give Mary another scholarship to attend the Moody Institute in Chicago, a school for Bible education and service being organized by evangelist Dwight L. Moody. On her application, Mary wrote that she wanted, more than anything, to train for missionary service.

For the first time in her life, Mary was the only Negro among white girls. But she soon forgot that difference and became invested in learning the Bible and evangelizing on the streets. Mary would deliver talks in the Pacific Garden Mission on Clark Street and sometimes sing from the Sankey Hymnal to the policemen and inmates at the jail. She visited the slums and what they called "skid row"—to the poorest of the city.[8] At Moody, Mary Jane discovered that she had a beautiful voice and was asked to join the Moody choir. Her teacher, listening to Mary Jane sing the hymn "My Faith Looks Up to Thee," said, "Mary, you always touch people to the quick. Maybe it's because your voice matches your heart."[9] As a member of the choir, she toured the northwestern United States.

Mary was able to meet Mr. Moody, who would visit the school in between evangelistic tours. She liked his kindly face and approachable manner. Once, she was asked to visit his office where he inquired about the conditions in the South among her people.[10]

Mary Jane McLeod had left behind the cotton fields of South Carolina. She had learned to read and write and sing. She was following God's calling on her life. Everything seemed to be going in the right direction . . . until graduation in 1895.

After completing her one-year study at Moody and filling out the application for missionary service, she received stunning news. The mission board where she had applied stated that they had no openings for Negro women in Africa. Mary sat in her dormitory room, refusing to allow tears to form. As she had done so often before, she turned to God in prayer.

"Whenever the Lord says no to me," said Mary, "I look into my heart and search my motives. For it is only the selfless me that God can use. At Moody, I saw that part of my wanting to go to Africa was a desire for travel. So I gave it up."[11]

Mary Jane refused to look back. She would continue to follow her God. He had provided a way out of the cotton fields, and He would certainly open a new door so she could serve Him.

CHAPTER TWENTY-SIX

Florida: The New Africa

An overturned apple barrel stood at the back of the room. It would serve as her makeshift desk. Late at night she had thought of an idea of using peach crates to make desks for her students. Mary surveyed the tiny room with satisfaction. Her dream of opening a school was becoming a reality.

When she rang the small bell clasped in the palm of her hand, five little girls would enter her classroom. And when she taught them how to read, their lives would change forever. She truly believed that education was the key to changing the future of the American Negro. With faith and education, she could make a difference in their lives—just like it had made a difference in hers.

A wealthy donor, James Gamble, hearing about Mary McLeod's work and vision, had paid a visit to her fledgling school. The man had looked with surprise at the old, broken-down furniture.

"Where," Gamble asked, "is this school you want me to be a trustee of?"

Mary looked directly into the eyes of the wealthy gentleman standing before her.

"In my mind," she replied, "and in my soul."[12]

Years earlier, refusing to be discouraged by the closed door to mission-ary service in Africa, Mary McLeod used her education and biblical training to teach at the Haines Institute in Augusta, Georgia. There, in 1898, she met and married a fellow teacher, a handsome, shy young man, named Al-bertus Bethune. Together, they had one child, a son.

Mary was content with this new opportunity and life settled into a pleasant routine of work and mothering. But somehow she couldn't shake a restless feeling that God was calling her to do more. Her husband dis-missed this as foolishness, but Mary felt the urge to move further south, to do more to meet the needs of her people. Packing up once again, the young couple traveled to Palatka, Florida, in 1899, where Mary became an instructor at the Palatka Mission School.

In Florida, during those years, there were increasing numbers of black workers moving south to build the Florida East Coast Railroad. Meanwhile, their families were living in squalor and children had no opportunities for school. Mary's heart ached, remembering the poverty of her own childhood and the lack of education she had experienced.

One day, she was talking to Reverend Pratt, a Methodist minister who worked with her at the Palatka Mission School, about the situation of the Negroes in Florida. The pastor handed her a bell and said, "I want you to go up there and ring up a school."[13]

His words challenged her heart, and she did just that. She rang her bell in Daytona Beach, Florida, an area where she saw the greatest need. She decided to start her own school . . . a school where black girls could learn to read, just as well as white children. In 1904, with just $1.65 in her pocket, she moved to Daytona. She approached the owner of an empty broken-down cottage on Oak Street that was renting for $11 a month. Mary told him that she only had $1.65 to her name, but that she would have that money by the end of the month. He agreed. Hoping for a bright future, she carved the name "Faith Hall" over the doorway.[14]

She furnished her small school with items she found in the trash bins behind the wealthy tourist hotels—scouring rubbish piles for cracked dishes and broken furniture. She made pencils from charred wood and ink from wild elderberry juice.[15] She recruited five girls to attend, and they were charged fifty cents a week. She taught them industrial skills, like sewing and housekeeping, but also how to read, write, and sing.

Mary named her school the Daytona Normal and Industrial School for Girls—and finally felt the satisfaction of seeing one of her life dreams become reality. When the first cabin became overcrowded, she went in search of vacant land. She found a spot nicknamed "Hell Hole" and paid five dollars for a down payment. It was the city's old dumping grounds, but Mary was unfazed.

To raise funds, Mary sold sweet potato pies and fried fish to Daytona Beach residents and tourists. She used her beautiful voice to entertain wealthy visitors in hotels and, when necessary, stood on the street corners and just begged. People laughed at her, calling her a dreamer. Undaunted by ridicule, Mary McLeod Bethune went on her way and "blacks and whites gathered under her banner."[16]

"Often I thank God for my rugged ways," Mary would later reflect. "Have not my people come over a way that with tears has been watered? But we are stronger today through the struggles with overcoming. I am stronger today because as I have taken the steep, hard way, I have taken time to be faithful, persevering and hopeful."[17]

Mary's vision attracted attention from wealthy donors who admired her brave spirit and supported the work with financial gifts and material donations. Two of those donors, James Gamble and Thomas H. White, became key supporters and friends. White eventually donated funds to build a dormitory and classroom building that is still named after him today: Whitehall.

She envisioned a better life for her students. On the blackboard of her classroom she chalked the words that would become one of her values: "Cease to be a drudge. Begin to be an artist."[18] She wanted the ambitions of her students to rise above and beyond mere service work that was common for her race.

In less than two years, her school had grown to include 250 students and four teachers. In those early years, money was still scarce. She fed her own family on black-eyed peas and hominy grits, putting every spare penny into the school.[19] Yet, she had seen God meet every need. When grocery bills couldn't be paid, a visitor would stop by with an unexpected check. When they had no dishes on which to eat, one of her wealthy donors would drop off a box of china. Each small donation was a miracle.

While the school was a success, her activities were also drawing controversy—many white residents were scandalized by her efforts to educate Negroes. Mary argued that they should be pleased that the people serving them were well educated—they did better work. One night, the school was visited by the Ku Klux Klan. They came in darkness, wearing hoods, carrying guns, and riding horses, terrorizing the neighborhood while warning Negroes not to vote.

Although her girls were frightened, Mary McLeod Bethune stood firm. She ordered that lights across the campus be turned on, shining brightly so the angry men could not hide. She told her students to sing. Quietly at first, and then more boldly, following Mary's lead, they sang: "Be not dismayed, whate'er betide, God will take care of you."

"We sang them right off campus," said Mary, "and the next day we all voted, too!"[19]

Mary's efforts extended beyond her students and into the community. One biographer wrote, "Mary McLeod Bethune lived in a racist society and had to accommodate to this reality."[20] She reports that in 1920, when women were first allowed to vote, Mary helped get 460 area black women registered—despite intimidation by the KKK. That same year, only 488 white women in the Daytona Beach area registered to vote.[21]

Even as her stature grew, she faced continued incidents of racial discrimination. One day, one of her students broke her arm. Mary took her to a doctor's home just across the river. A nurse, answering the door, told her, "You'll have to go around to the back door." Mary refused. This strengthened her determination to build a hospital for Negroes in her community.[22]

Despite the oppressive attitude toward her people, Mary remained positive and resolute. She believed that God had sent her to Florida, her "new Africa" and that He would continue to provide a way. She loved what she was doing and believed in her calling.

God had sent her here—and God would provide a way.

CHAPTER TWENTY-SEVEN

A Legacy of Hope

<p>raffic in the nation's capital rushed frantically forward, horns honking and people bustling by, nothing like the slow, leisurely pace of Florida. Mary approached an empty taxicab to take her to the White House, but the driver turned, looked at Mary, and shook his head with a decisive "no."

Mary opened the cab door anyway, and took her seat.

"This cab is empty," she told the driver. "Why did you tell me I couldn't enter."

"I don't drive Negroes," replied the man.

"Well, you're driving me," said Dr. Mary McLeod Bethune.

As the driver started up the vehicle and headed to her destination, Mary talked to the man about his feelings of prejudice toward African-Americans. Why did he assume that all Negroes would cause him harm? Did he realize that Negroes, like white people, were individuals? Why would he deny services to an entire race?

She then explained to him who she was, an official of the United States government, appointed to office by the president.

The man apologized. He would never forget his conversation with Dr. Mary McLeod Bethune.

After its humble beginning, Mary's Florida school had continued to grow. They had begun to offer high school courses and then had developed into a junior college. In 1923, the school merged with Cookman Institute (an all-boys school) and began to train both young men and women. Yet it held true to its values—teaching God's truth as well as practical and academic skills to students.[23]

In addition, Mary McLeod Bethune had impacted the surrounding community. She had developed a hospital and held classes for married couples—teaching homemaking and family-development skills. She had worked hard to teach Negroes to read and to gain them access to vote. And, in the midst of all of this, she continued to fund-raise. She would approach any person, white or black, wealthy or not, to tell them of her work and the importance of supporting education and training for American Negroes. She traveled across the state and the nation, telling of the work being done in Florida and encouraging other schools to join her in providing education and hope to African Americans.

Her home life had been less successful. Albert, failing to understand or sympathize with the time and energy she poured into educating young women, had left her and their son and returned to South Carolina. In 1918, he died. Although certainly dismayed at this turn of events, Mary had refused to lose focus on her goals.[24]

Her work did not go unnoticed. One day, she received a call from the White House asking her to attend a Child Welfare Conference held by President Calvin Coolidge. What an unexpected honor! That first visit to Washington was intimidating and exciting for Mary, and her first stop was New York to purchase a new outfit for the occasion. She purchased a fur "marten" scarf—something she had never owned before. Here she was, the same Mary who had once picked cotton in a field, now being asked to appear before the president![25]

At the White House, the meeting room was crowded with educators and child welfare experts. Each person was asked to briefly report on the state of the children in their area of service. While the meeting was brief, and her interaction with the president minimal, it was only a beginning. From that point on, Mary McLeod Bethune was frequently called upon by the government to report on and move forward the work of racial reconciliation in the United States.

In the 1930s, the nation was rocked by the Great Depression. This had an enormous effect on young people. Juvenile delinquency was at an all-time high and depression and despair characterized the nation's youth. In 1934, President Franklin Delano Roosevelt called a meeting of outstanding Americans to address the problem.[26] Mary McLeod Bethune was on his list of people to attend.

By that time, Mary's social and political achievements were getting noticed. She had been given numerous academic and political honors including one from the NAACP—the Joel E. Spingarn gold medal "for the highest and noblest achievement of an American Negro."

In 1935, she attended a meeting at the White House where she met Franklin Roosevelt. She felt an immediate close connection to the friendly, dignified man. He looked her straight in the eye, shook her hand, smiled, and said, "How do you do, Mrs. Bethune. I know you."

She felt the same way. They shared an immediate bond and a common concern for the fate of all young people of the land, no matter what their race. Mary told the president about the plight of the American Negro—particularly the youth. She explained to the president that fifteen or twenty dollars would make a real difference in the life of the average minority student. What might be entertainment money to other teens would be used by her students to pay doctors' bills and buy books. "We are bringing life and spirit to these many thousands who have lived in darkness!" said Mary.[27]

She asked President Roosevelt to use his influence to help change the life of the American Negro. After her impassioned speech, the president had tears in his eyes and offered his sincere appreciation. Shortly after returning home, she received a letter from the White House asking her to accept a newly created position as the administrator of the Office of Minority Affairs.

Mary was torn. She felt she was needed in Florida. Yet, she realized this was a significant appointment. She would be the first Negro woman to have a federal position created on her behalf. She accepted. That decision became the first of many personal encounters and a deep friendship with the president and his wife, Eleanor. She was often called to sit in his office, across his desk, and share the burdens of her heart. When he died, he left her his silver-tipped cane, engraved with his initials F.D.R.

He said of her, "Mrs. Bethune is a great woman. I believe in her because she has her feet on the ground—not only on the ground but in the deep, plowed soil."[28]

In 1930, during a convention of the National Association for Colored Women in California, Mary paid a visit to a woman from her past, Miss Mary Chrissman. Over the years, she had kept up a correspondence with the donor who had given money as a scholarship to begin her education. As the two women met, after so many years, they both had tears in their eyes. Miss Chrissman saw before her a strong, confident woman, a far cry from the little girl working in the cotton patch.

That night, Mary honored her friend in a speech: "My dear Miss Chrissman, the hundreds of women you are seeing here, and the thousands over America and the isles of the sea, are clipping coupons on your investment in me.

> "My dear Miss Chrissman, the hundreds of women you are seeing here, and the thousands over America and the isles of the sea, are clipping coupons on your investment in me."

"If you had not sacrificed, no leadership would have been vouchsafed to me. If it were not for you and others of similar generosity, few would be here today to render beautiful service in their turn. Please accept this tribute with prayers on our lips, that God may grant you many more years, and that others like you may be raised to carry on His work."[29]

Mary's work with President Roosevelt was the beginning of a long and significant career of government service. She was Director of Negro Affairs for the National Youth Administration from 1936 to 1944. She served as Special Adviser to the President on Minority Affairs from 1936–1944. She was the Special Assistant to the Secretary of War for Selection of Candidates in 1942, helping to open the door for Negroes in WAACS and WAVES. She was named a general in the Woman's Army for National Defense.[30]

Mary McLeod Bethune organized one million Negro women into the National Council of Negro Women in order that they could have proper representation in War and Defense. She drew together African Americans to have a solid, unified voice—allowing them to speak boldly and to address the needs of their people during the tumultuous years of desegregation.[31]

In 1953, one of Mary's dearest dreams came true. She was asked to go to Africa, to Liberia, as a part of a special team of United States representatives for the inauguration of their president. Years earlier, as a young woman, she had applied to go to Africa as a missionary and was denied. Now, as her feet touched the African soil, she was in her seventies and traveling to Africa in a position of honor.

As she neared her final years, Mary McLeod Bethune transitioned to the role of president emeritus of Bethune Cookman and handed over the leadership of her life's work. She was not able to travel as much as she had in the past. She knew she was slowing down.

She sat in the breakfast nook at her home remembering how, when she was a little girl, she had longed for a home with real glass windows. How far she had come! Contemplating her legacy, she decided to leave her home, not to her heirs, but to a foundation that would showcase the collection of her lifetime. She wanted it to be a place of inspiration for others—the demonstration of how dreams can become reality. Mary wrote:

> When I wake up in the morning and look around, see my glass windows, I see my Bible on the table, see the rug on my floor, my bathroom, my bathtub, I have a thanksgiving in my heart for what God has done for me.
>
> So I want this always to be kind of a sacred place—a place to awaken people and to have them realize there is something in the world they can do; and if they try hard enough, they will do that thing. [32]

She also published her last will and testament, copies of which are still distributed to students at her college today. The will did not dispense her worldly possessions, but offered hope and love and wisdom for the future. She wrote:

> I leave you love. Love builds. It is positive and helpful. It is more beneficial than hate. Injuries quickly forgotten quickly pass away. Personally and racially, our enemies must be forgiven. Our aim must be to create a world of fellowship and justice where no man's skin, color or religion, is held against him.
>
> "Love thy neighbor" is a precept which could transform the world.

On May 18, 1955, Dr. Mary McLeod Bethune died at her home in Daytona Beach, Florida. As she entered her heavenly home, she left behind a legacy of faith, hope, and courage. She was later recognized as one of the most influential African-American women in the United States and given a postage stamp in her honor.

She wrote:

> As I face tomorrow, I am content, for I think I have spent my life well. I pray now that my philosophy may be helpful to those who share my vision of a world of Peace, Progress, Brotherhood, and Love. [33]

Being That Kind of Woman

I am aware, as I close this book, that I have only scratched the surface. There are many more women whose stories are not included that deserve to be told. They, too, followed God's leading and ventured into unknown places to serve Him. We need to share these stories. We need to encourage one another in our faith. We need to influence society as Christians and as women. We need to pass on our faith, in a rich and meaningful way, to the younger generation of women.

But, even more, *we* need to be that kind of woman. We need to be women who do not "shudder" in the face of fearful or uncomfortable situations, but who do the right thing and bravely step forward in faith.

These women taught me that being a woman of faith is not always easy, but it is always rewarding. They showed me that each of us has an individual path to follow—no two look the same. While the stories of these eight women are definitely unique, they also have a great deal in common. Their lives show us what it actually looks like to be a follower of Jesus Christ. These women:

1) **Experienced hardship.** Many of them had physical difficulties that could have severely limited their ability to serve God well. Fanny grew up without sight. Nettie lost her hearing. Others saw their marriages

crumble or children become ill. It is easy to let the ordinary trials of life devastate us and consume our energy. We may feel that we have little time left to reach out to others. Some days, it may seem that all we can do is cope. Throughout these stories, these women cried out to God in their times of need and distress. They did not ignore their troubles, but they did not let the hard things of life stop them, either. God used each of them, despite their difficult personal circumstances. Sometimes, I think He even used those situations to propel them into ministry.

2) **Served with faithfulness.** When I think of faithfulness, I see Sarah Dunn Clarke sitting on the platform of the Pacific Garden Mission, night after night. In the beginning, she was young and married, most likely full of energy and vision. At the end, she was older and widowed. She was probably physically tired and certainly lonely. But Sarah didn't let those feelings stop her. She served daily. She got up each day determined to fulfill her duty. Each night, she sat on the platform—quietly doing what she believed God had asked her to do. She didn't do this to earn personal acclaim. She was just following Jesus. It is easy, in our modern day world, to stop and start our commitments. I learned, through Sarah, that type of daily commitment counts. God needs faithful servants who refuse to drop out.

3) **Bravely faced opposition.** I will always picture Mary McLeod Bethune shaking her fist at the Ku Klux Klan and marching them right off of her Florida campus. I cannot even begin to imagine how her heart pounded at the sight of the hooded men on horseback approaching. Young girls clung to her and hid behind her. She was not a small woman, but she was no match for this group of burly, hateful men. I love how she refused to back down. She did not shudder. She lit the lights and led the students in a hymn. They would sing those evil men right off the campus. Whether we are called to stand up to the forces of hatred, like Mary McLeod Bethune, or stand up for our ideas, like Emma Dryer, I believe

there are situations that call us to be firm and resolute. We have God on our side. He has promised to be with us not just in easy times, but in battle. These women refused to shrink away from conflict.

4) **Ignored societal rules.** Virginia Asher probably caused more than a few eyebrows to rise when she walked into Chicago's brothel district and sat down to pray with a prostitute. Her love for Christ and His people extended into some of the darkest parts of the city—places where no "respectable" people would go—or at least did not go openly. She and her husband evangelized in saloons and she passed out pamphlets in the seedy atmosphere of the World's Fair. She was most likely criticized by others in the faith who thought she was inviting scandal. She risked her personal reputation for Jesus. The societal rules may have changed, but there are still parts of our communities that would be considered off-limits for "good Christian women."

5) **Found their value in Christ alone.** When Sarah Dunn Clarke gave up her jewels and left her affluent home, she knew she was making a choice that would determine her life's future. On the opposite side, Amanda Berry Smith, who grew up with nothing and endured the injustice of slavery and prejudice, knew that she was precious in God's sight. Each woman learned that her value was not determined by her economic circumstance or the color of her skin. We are not more important to God if we are born wealthy or in the most desperate of circumstances. We are equally free and justified and redeemed by Him. We are His children and He is our Heavenly Father. That knowledge sets us all free. It enables us to rise up beyond our life circumstances and to take risks we might not even think possible.

In each of these eight stories, the women had minds that were made up—they had decided that their goal was worth the risk. They moved forward, stepping out in faith, in small and big ways, and made an eternal difference.

On the gravestones of the women in these books, their epigraphs are simple. They have unpretentious statements like, "She hath done what she could," or "She has given her best that others may live a more abundant life." In their words, you can see that they did not set out to achieve great fame or to make history books. They just wanted to serve God well.

"She hath done what she could."

Have we?

Have you?

We must refuse to shudder in the face of hardship. We must be faithful to serve even when we are tired and the days seem long. We must resist the urge to let our life circumstances and personal weaknesses limit our ability to serve God. We must refuse to find value in what we wear or the beauty of our home. We must let our reputation rest in Him and not in the eyes of society. We must follow God as He leads, each simple step of the way, as He transforms our ordinary lives into remarkable ones.

I hope the stories of these eight women will encourage your heart and renew your vision for what God can and will do through your life. It is so easy to get caught up in the daily routine and let the normal duties of our lives claim all of our energy and attention. But if God is tugging at your heart and showing you a way that you can serve Him, you must pay attention. Listen to His voice. Know that He views your life as unique, important, and powerful. He will use you in ways you can't imagine.

If we place our faith in Him daily, I am certain that God can and will use our simple, ordinary, wonderful lives, and the opportunities and talents that He has given uniquely to each of us, to do extraordinary things for His glory.

FOR FURTHER DISCUSSION

FANNY CROSBY

1) Even as a child, Fanny Crosby refused to be limited by what she could not do—see. What are the things you have been unable to do in life? Do you think they have limited your ability to live a full life? Why or why not?

2) Fanny took a big risk when she left the comfort of her home and traveled to the New York Institution for the Blind. What is the biggest risk you have taken in life? Did it pay off? Was leaving your comfort zone worthwhile in the end?

3) Fanny fell in love and married, but was disappointed in her relationship with Van. Why do you think her marriage was not successful? Is happiness in love a guarantee for believers? How does it influence our work for God?

EMMA DRYER

1) Women of Emma Dryer's day were expected to marry and devote their life to household work. What are the social expectations for women today? Are they different for Christian women? How has your life conformed to or gone against the expectations of society or the church?

2) Emma had a "mercurial" temper. She was known for being overly critical. In many ways, it was the flipside of her strengths, such as her attention to detail and her unfailing commitment. What are your weaknesses? Are your weaknesses connected to your strengths?

3) Women, both single and married, often struggle with loneliness. Why do you think this is so common? What can we do when we are struck by periods of depression or loneliness?

NETTIE McCORMICK

1) Nettie was married to a wealthy, powerful man. Yet, this marriage also came with the cost of loneliness. If you are married, what have been the "costs" of that decision? On the positive side, what has been one of the rewards?

2) Mental illness is prevalent in today's society. Two of Nettie's children were afflicted with this heavy burden. How do we help those who are struggling with mental illness? How can our faith help us navigate issues like these when they strike our family and loved ones?

3) Nettie McCormick and Emma Dryer were close friends—but very different in their background and personalities. Do you have a friend like that? Are you more different or alike? How do your differences benefit your friendship?

SARAH DUNN CLARKE

1) Sarah was struck by God speaking to her, asking, "What are you doing to decorate your heavenly home?" In our culture, it is not uncommon for women to become obsessed with home décor and cooking. We exchange recipes and crafting ideas on Pinterest and other social media sites. How might our domestic obsessions limit our impact for God? Or can we use them for Him?

2) The Clarkes experienced a miraculous answer to their prayers for funding. Have you ever prayed for something and experienced God's answer? If not, why do you think we often hesitate to pray for our personal needs?

3) Sarah was at the mission day after day—never missing a session. How did that extreme level of faithfulness contribute to her service? Think of a woman you know who serves quietly and faithfully. Why is it difficult to serve in that way?

AMANDA SMITH

1) Amanda Smith felt completely alone following the death of her baby, Will. At that very moment, God sent a friend to give her needed money. Why are women's friendships so crucial? How have friends ministered to you in times of need?

2) Slavery left a deep wound upon the African Americans in our country and segregation prolonged that pain. How can women in the church work toward reconciliation between the races? What can we learn from Amanda Smith's story and her positive attitude toward faith and life?

3) Amanda was asked, at one point, to write her life story. This was a difficult task for her, but she did it to inspire others. Have you ever attempted to write the story of your faith? Have you been inspired by the biographies or stories of other Christian women?

VIRGINIA ASHER

1) Virginia lost her first child. Many women today have suffered miscarriages or lost a baby shortly after birth. Others, who deeply desire children, find they are infertile. Why is our ability to have children so closely linked to our personal identity? What is particularly painful about this type of loss for women? Can God use this common point in our lives?

2) For Virginia, ministry meant going into places considered "unsavory" at the time: brothels and saloons. Yet, she went anyway, risking her personal reputation to share God's love. What sorts of places are considered

off-limits in our society? Have you tried to cross those boundaries? What was the response?

3) Through her business councils, Virginia tried to pass on the "torch" to a younger generation. She inspired many younger women to serve God. How can women today influence younger women to follow God?

EVANGELINE BOOTH

1) At a young age, Evangeline decided to remain single to better serve God. Many could not understand her decision, and she continued to receive proposals from men wanting her to consider marriage. Do you think singleness is a good option for women in ministry? What are the rewards of this choice? Is it still controversial?

2) Evangeline's hymn "The World for God" speaks of the vast needs in our world today. What world events have broken your heart in recent days? What part of the world have you been burdened to reach for God?

3) Evangeline was known for her Quaker style "uniform"—a bonnet and dark dress. What is the Christian woman's "uniform" today? How does our choice of clothing influence our ability to minister? Should it?

MARY MCLEOD BETHUNE

1) Mary was born into slavery and limited in her ability to gain an education. For her, achievement meant someday having a home with glass windows. What object or event represents achieving your goals and dreams? Why?

2) Mary had one door shut firmly in her face. She had trained to go to Africa as a missionary and then was rejected because of her race. Instead of becoming bitter at this unjustly closed door, she moved to Florida and began

a school. How have shut doors in your own life opened up other opportunities? Do you believe God works in this way?

3) Mary bravely faced off against prejudice—in the forms of the Ku Klux Klan and in the quieter avoidance of the Washington cab driver. Have you experienced prejudice? How did you react? How can we combat prejudice in a godly way?

4) Miss Chrissman, through her donations, paid for Mary's schooling. Years later, Mary went to find her and thank her for her gift. Who has contributed to your life and faith? How might you express your thanks for those gifts?

ACKNOWLEDGMENTS

No book is written by just one person. As I write these words, I am humbly aware of so many who have contributed to this project.

First, to each of these eight women—this book is about them and because of them. I want the honor to land firmly at their feet, for they are the ones who walked the long and difficult road of faithful service. They have my utmost admiration. I hope to be just a bit like them.

Second, I am thankful to the marvelous, encouraging editors at Moody Publishers. Holly Kisly—you believed in this project from the start and understood how important it was to tell these stories to women. Karen Waddles—I have appreciated both your affirmation and your thoughtful editorial revisions. Pam Pugh—thank you for your close, careful eye that helped redeem my research errors. I deeply appreciate these women who contributed to my research: Dawn Pulgine, Amy Koehler, Allana Pierce, Carol Forbes, and Nikki Tochalauski. Special thanks to my audience development manager, Rene Hanebutt, who captured the very spirit of this book with its creative packaging. The illustrated cover art is by the gifted Jonathan Critcher, and my author photo is the work of my talented and generous dear friend Jill Obermaier.

To the men and women at each of these organizations who continue to do God's work today: Thank you for your assistance in this project, but most importantly for carrying on the rich legacy these women leave behind. The Salvation Army, The Pacific Garden Mission, The Moody Bible Institute, and Bethune-Cookman University and Mary McLeod Bethune Foundation deserve our support and prayers.

Thank you to those who have inspired me, both as a writer and as a woman. I would begin to list them, but I am fearful of leaving anyone out of this long, long list. You are my friends, my teachers, my mentors, my students, my colleagues. You have poured into my life in rich and lasting ways.

To my family, each and every one of you, and to my husband, Milt, thank you for believing in me and for the love and laughter you bring to my life. And finally, to my daughter, Sabrina Rose, I believe you are a great woman. I am honored to be your mom.

To God be the glory, great things He has done!

NOTES

Introduction: They Refused to Give Up

1. Lorraine Hansberry, *To Be Young, Gifted and Black* (New York: Penguin, 1970).

Chapters 1–3: Fanny Crosby

1. Fanny Crosby, *Memories of Eighty Years* (Boston: J.H. Early & Co, 1906), 19.

2. Ibid., 18.

3. Ibid., 18.

4. Ibid., 25.

5. Ibid., 26.

6. Ibid., 29

7. Ibid., 37.

8. Ibid., 37.

9. Ibid., 38

10. This little "place in the country" is now located near Ninth Avenue and 34th Street in urban New York City. Current maps show the school's location was between the Lincoln Tunnel and Madison Square Garden in the now bustling and pricey Manhattan. Michael C. Mellox, "One Hundred Years of Education of the Blind in America," *The New York Institute for Special Education*, 2007.

11. Crosby, *Memories of Eighty Years*, 42.

12. Mary E. Rogers, "Fanny Crosby: The Early Years," *The Mentor*, Vol. 2:2 (1892).

13. Crosby, *Memories of Eighty Years*, 45.

14. Louis W. Rodenburg, "The Song Bird in the Dark," *Outlook for the Blind* 25: Dec. 1931, 155–160.

15. Ibid.

16. J. Reginald Casswell, *Fanny Crosby: The Sightless Songstress* (London, Pickering & Inglis), 27.

17. Rodenburg, "The Song Bird in the Dark."

18. Crosby, *Memories of Eighty Years*, 97.

19. Fanny Crosby, *Fanny Crosby's Life-Story* (New York: Every Where Publishing Company, 1903), 43.

20. Rodenburg, "The Song Bird in the Dark."

21. Ibid.

22. Crosby, *Fanny Crosby's Life-Story*, 56.

23. Ibid, 56.

24. Edith L. Blumhofer, *Her Heart Can See: The Life and Hymns of Fanny J. Crosby* (Grand Rapids: Wm. B. Eerdmans, 2005), 176.

25. Crosby, *Fanny Crosby's Life-Story*, 57.

26. Blumhofer, *Her Heart Can See: The Life and Hymns of Fanny J. Crosby*, 310.

27. Ibid., 312.

28. Ibid., 314.

29. "The History of the Bowery Mission," The Bowery Mission, 2010, http://www.bowery.org/about-us/history/.

30. Crosby, *Memories of Eighty Years*, 145.

31. Fanny Crosby, "Rescue the Perishing," Lyrics, 1869.

32. Crosby, *Memories of Eighty Years*, 156.

33. Ibid., 167.

34. Ibid.

35. Blumhofer, *Her Heart Can See: The Life and Hymns of Fanny J. Crosby*, 284.

36. Ibid., 213.

37. Ibid., 214.

38. "Frances Jane Van Alystyne (Fanny Crosby) 1820–1915 Hymn Writer," Faith Hall of Fame, European-American Evangelistic Crusades, http://www.eaec.org/faithhallfame/fanny_crosby.htm.

39. Ibid.

40. Blumhofer, *Her Heart Can See: The Life and Hymns of Fanny J. Crosby*, 229.

41. Ibid., 312.

42. "5000 Sing with Blind Hymn Writer: Fanny Crosby, Now, 91, Rouses Evangelistic Rally in Carnegie Hall," *New York Times Archives* (May 3, 1911).

43. Crosby, *Fanny Crosby's Life-Story*, 172.

44. Rodenburg, "The Song Bird in the Dark."

45. Ibid., 47.

46. Blumhofer, *Her Heart Can See: The Life and Hymns of Fanny J. Crosby*, 338.

47. "Fanny Crosby, Blind Hymn Writer, Dies." *New York Times*, 13 Feb. 1915.

48. Moseley H. Williams, "The Man Born Blind," *The Sunday-School World*, Vol. 40:8, *American Sunday School Union*, August 1900. Google Books.

Chapters 4–6: "Emma" Emeline E Dryer

1. Cynthia L. Ogorek, "Emma Dryer," *Women Building Chicago: 1790–1990*, Rima Lynn Schultz and Adele Hast, eds. (Indiana University Press, 2001), 230.

2. "Ingham University: 1837-1892)," Woodward Memorial Library, http://www.wood-wardmemoriallibrary.org/university.php.

3. Ogorek, "Emma Dryer," 230.

4. Ibid.

5. "Early College Women Determined to be Educated," *Women of Courage* profile series, St. Lawrence County, NY: American Association of University Women, Oct. 20, 2012.

6. Emma Dryer, "Letter to President Blanchard," January 1916, Biographical Files, Moody Bible Institute, Chicago.

7. Dennis McClendon, "Chicago Growth 1850-1890," University of Illinois Chicago, http://tigger.uic.edu/depts/ahaa/imagebase/chimaps/mcclendon.

8. Ogorek, "Emma Dryer," 230.

9. Dryer, "Letter to President Blanchard," January 1916.

10. Ogorek, "Emma Dryer," Women Building Chicago: 1790-1990, Rima Lynn Schultz and Adele Hast, eds, (Indiana University Press, 2001), 230.

11. Lowell K. Handy, "Bible Study and the Moody Bible Institute: From Dryer to Peterman," Paper for Chicago Society of Bible and Research, April 24, 2010, Biographical Files, Moody Bible Institute, Chicago.

12. Dryer, "Letter to President Blanchard," January 1916.

13. Lyle W. Dorsett, *A Passion for Souls: The Life of D.L. Moody* (Chicago: Moody, 1997), 64.

14. Ibid., 122.

15. Dryer, "Letter to President Blanchard," January 1916.

16. Ibid.

17. Ibid.

18. "The Great Chicago Fire," Chicago Historical Society, 1999. http://chicagohs.org/history/fire.html.

19. Emma Dryer, "Letter to Miss Waite," July 18, 1924, Emma Dryer, Biographical File, Moody Bible Institute, Chicago.

20. Ibid.

21. Dryer, "Letter to President Blanchard," January 1916.

22. Ibid.

23. Ibid.

24. Ibid.

25. Abraham Ruelas, "Women and the Landscape of American Higher Education: Wesleyan Holiness and Pentecostal Founders," Presentation for conference at Wesleyan Theological Society and the Society for Pentecostal Studies, 2009.

26. *Sixty-Second Annual Report of the Chicago Bible Society for the Year 1901*, Chicago, January 27, 1902, Biographical Files, Moody Bible Institute, Chicago.

27. Rosemary Rausch and Chris Snyder, "Three Women in the Life of D.L. Moody," Moody Bible Institute, Chicago, Oct. 7, 1981, Biographical Files, Moody Bible Institute, Chicago.

28. Dryer, "Letter to President Blanchard," January 1916.

29. Dryer, "Letter to Miss Waite," July 18, 1924.

30. Ibid.

31. Dryer, "Letter to President Blanchard," January 1916.

32. Ibid.

33. Emma Dryer, "Letter to Mrs. Nettie McCormick," Letters to Mrs. McCormick, Moody Bible Institute, Chicago.

34. Dryer, "Letter to President Blanchard," January 1916.

35. Dorsett, *A Passion for Souls: The Life of D.L. Moody*, 275–77.

36. Ibid., 273.

37. Dryer, "Letter to President Blanchard," January 1916.

38. Ibid.

39. Ibid.

40. Rausch and Snyder, "Three Women in the Life of D.L. Moody."

41. Dryer, "Letter to President Blanchard," January 1916.

42. Emma MacNaughton, "Letter to Dr. Wilbur Smith," 1945, Emma Dryer, Biographical File, Moody Bible Institute, Chicago.

43. Emma Dryer, "Letter to D.L. Moody," July 25, 1887, Emma Dryer, Biographical File, Moody Bible Institute, Chicago

44. Ibid.

45. Ogorek, "Emma Dryer."

46. *Sixty-Second Annual Report of the Chicago Bible Society for the Year 1901*.

47. Ibid.

48. W.H. Gaylord, "Letter to Miss Waite." April 22, 1926, Emma Dryer, Biographical Files, Moody Bible Institute, Chicago.

49. *Sixty-Second Annual Report of the Chicago Bible Society for the Year 1901*.

50. MacNaughton, "Letter to Dr. Wilbur Smith," 1945.

51. "Emma Dryer," Moody Bible Institute Website, Library, Biographies.

Chapter 7: Women and Education

1. "Illegal to Teach Slaves to Read and Write." *Harpers Weekly*, June 21, 1862, http://www.sonofthesouth.net/leefoundaiton/civil-war/1862/june/slaves-read-write.htm.

2. Maggie Lowe, "Early College Women: Determined to Be Educated," Woman of Courage profile, St. Lawrence County, NY Branch of the American Association of University Women, http://www.northnet.org/stlawrenceaauw/college.htm.

3. "St. Mary's School," Knox County Historical Sites, Inc., http://www.kville.org/kchistory/About.html.

4. Lowe, "Early College Women: Determined to be Educated."

5. Ibid.

Chapters 8–10: "Nettie" Nancy (Fowler) McCormick

1. "Nettie McCormick," http://www.Christianity.com.

2. Lawrence P. Gooley, "Noted Local Philanthropist Nettie McCormick," *The Adirondack Almanack*, ," 28 Nov. 2011, http://

3. Ibid.

4. "Schooling," Virginia Roderick Papers (Comments, Outlines, Sources), Nettie Fowler McCormick Biographical Association Administrative File, Nettie McCormick Papers, Wisconsin Historical Society Archives.

5. Ibid.

6. "Courtship and Marriage," Virginia Roderick Papers (Comments, Outlines, Sources), Nettie Fowler McCormick Biographical Association Administrative File, Nettie McCormick Papers, Wisconsin Historical Society Archives.

7. Ibid.

8. Ibid.

9. "Interview with Mr. and Mrs. Truman B. Gorton at the Lawson Young Men's Christian Association of Chicago," Sept. 23, 1933, Virginia Roderick Papers (Comments, Outlines, Sources), Nettie Fowler McCormick Biographical Association Administrative File, Nettie McCormick Papers, Wisconsin Historical Society Archives.

10. "Nettie McCormick," http://www.Christianity.com.

11. Ibid.

12. Ibid.

13. "Interview with Mrs. Morrill Dunn," Interviews and Recollections: Dunn, Mrs. Morrill to Lyons, John F. June 29, 1933, Nettie McCormick Papers, Wisconsin Historical Society Archives.

14. Ibid.

15. Ibid.

16. "Nettie McCormick," http://www.Christianity.com.

17. "Mrs. Cyrus Hall McCormick," *National Cyclopaiedia of American Biography* 31 (1931), Mead Project Web. Jan. 15, 2013, 80–81.

18. Kevin Davis, "McCormicks," Encyclopedia of Chicago, http://www.encyclopedia.chicagohistory.org/pages/2204.html.

19. Nettie McCormick, "Letter to Sarah Dunn Clarke," n.d., Nettie McCormick Papers, Wisconsin Historical Society Archives.

20. "Cyrus McCormick," Spiritus-Temporis, 2004, http://www.spiritus-temporis.com/cyrus-mccormick/death.html.

21. "Nettie McCormick," http://www.Christianity.com.

22. "Mrs. McCormick Leads Women on Tax Lists," *Chicago Daily News*, June 20, 1917. Cyrus H. McCormick Jr. Papers. Wisconsin Historical Society Archives.

23. "Interview with Geraldine Beeks Easley," Feb. 15, 1934. Nettie McCormick Papers, Wisconsin Historical Society Archives.

24. Emma Dryer, "Letter to Mrs. McCormick," Oct. 8, 1886, Nettie McCormick Papers, Wisconsin Historical Society Archives.

25. "Interview with Mr. A.F. Gaylord," Moody Bible Institute. Nov. 9, 1937. Virginia Roderick Papers. Nettie McCormick Papers, Wisconsin Historical Society Archives.

26. "Mother of the Seminary," Notes, Virginia Roderick Papers (Comments, Outlines, Sources), Nettie Fowler McCormick Papers, Wisconsin Historical Society Archives.

27. Ibid.

28. Ibid.

29. Ibid.

30. Ibid.

31. "Egypt," Notes, Virginia Roderick Papers, Nettie Fowler McCormick Papers, Wisconsin Historical Society Archives.

32. "Interview with Louise Yim Hahan," Mar. 9, 1939, Virginia Roderick Papers, Nettie Fowler McCormick Papers, Wisconsin Historical Society Archives.

33. "Interview with Mrs. Morrill Dunn," June 29, 1933.

34. "Memorandum on telephone talk with Anita B," Dec. 4, 1943, Virginia Roderick Papers, Nettie Fowler McCormick Papers, Wisconsin Historical Society Archives.

35. "Mrs. McCormick at 80 Gets a World Tribute," *Herald*, Feb. 9, 1915, Clippings, McCormick Collection, Cyrus H. McCormick Jr. Papers, McC Mss 2C Box No. 14, Wisconsin Historical Society Archives.

36. Ibid.

37. Ibid.

38. "Mrs. Cyrus Hall McCormick," *National Cyclopaedia of American Biography*, 31 (1931), 80–81.

⚶ NOTES ⚶

Chapters 11–13: Sarah Dunn Clarke

1. Carl F. Henry, *The Pacific Garden Mission: A Doorway to Heaven* (Grand Rapids: Zondervan, 1942), 79.

2. Sarah Dunn Clarke, *The Founding of the Pacific Garden Mission: Over Thirty-Five Years Contributed to the Master's Service* (Chicago: Bronson Printing Co, 1914), 11.

3. Ibid., 12.

4. Harold M. Mayer and Richard C. Wade, *Chicago: Growth of Metropolis* (Chicago: University of Chicago Press, 1973), 64.

5. Ibid., 66.

6. Clarke, *The Founding of the Pacific Garden Mission,* 15.

7. Ibid., 16.

8. David Lowe, *The Great Chicago Fire* (New York: Dover Publications, 1979) 22.

9. Mayer and Wade, *Chicago: Growth of Metropolis*, 117.

10. *The Way Out: Golden Anniversary of the Pacific Garden Mission: 1877–1927*, (Chicago, 1927), 5.

11. Karen Abbott, *Sin in the Second City* (New York: Random House, 2007), 10.

12. *The Way Out: Golden Anniversary of the Pacific Garden Mission: 1877–1927*, 6.

13. Ibid.

14. Henry, *The Pacific Garden Mission: A Doorway to Heaven*, 7.

15. Ibid.

16. Clarke, *The Founding of the Pacific Garden Mission,* 23.

17. Ibid., 24.

18. Henry, *The Pacific Garden Mission: A Doorway to Heaven*, 33.

19. Ibid., 32.

20. Clarke, *The Founding of the Pacific Garden Mission*, 56.

21. *The Way Out: Golden Anniversary of the Pacific Garden Mission: 1877–1927*, 11.

22. Clarke, *The Founding of the Pacific Garden Mission*, 27.

23. Ibid., 44–45.

24. Ibid., 29.

25. Henry, *The Pacific Garden Mission: A Doorway to Heaven*, 30.

26. Ibid., 3.

27. Ibid., 30.

28. Clarke, *The Founding of the Pacific Garden Mission*, 49.

29. Henry, *The Pacific Garden Mission: A Doorway to Heaven*, 80.

30. Ibid., 46.

31. *The Way Out: Golden Anniversary of the Pacific Garden Mission: 1877–1927*, 20–23.

32. Ibid., 24.

33. Ibid., 7.

34. Clarke, *The Founding of the Pacific Garden Mission*, 62–63.

35. Ibid., 79.

36. Ibid., 12.

37. Ibid., 33

38. *The Way Out: Golden Anniversary of the Pacific Garden Mission: 1877–1927*, 11.

Chapters 14–16: Amanda Smith

1. Amanda Smith, *An Autobiography: The Story of the Lord's Dealings with Mrs. Amanda Smith* (Chicago: Meyer and Brother, 1893), Electronic Edition, Academic Affairs Library, UNC-CH University of North Carolina at Chapel Hill, 1999.

2. Ibid., 26.

3. Scott Minugs, "Shrewsbury Black Man was Conductor on Underground Railroad," *Cannonball-York Blog* (Sept. 24, 2011).

4. Randy Pletzer, "Amanda Berry Smith: The African Sibyl," Journal of the Historical Society of the EPA Conference, 2011, 5.

5. Smith, *An Autobiography: The Story of the Lord's Dealings with Mrs. Amanda Smith*, 27.

6. Ibid., 30.

7. Maggie Maclean, "Amanda Smith: African American Evangelist and Missionary," Civil War Women Blog: Women of the Civil War and Reconstruction Eras 1849–1877 (Oct. 28, 2006).

8. Smith, *An Autobiography: The Story of the Lord's Dealings with Mrs. Amanda Smith*, 103.

9. Ibid., 59.

10. Ibid., 80.

11. Ibid., 123.

12. Ibid., 124.

13. Ibid., 170.

14. Ibid., 493.

15. Ibid., 196.

16. Ibid., 198

17. Ibid., 216.

18. Ibid., 264.

19. Ibid., vii.

20. Ibid., ix.

21. Ibid., 365.

22. Ibid., 389.

23. Ibid.

24. Ibid., 393

25. Ibid., 487.

26. Ibid., preface.

27. "T.W. Harvey," *The Institute Tie* (Nov 30, 1892) vol. 2, no. 2. Archives, Moody Bible Institute, Chicago, 1.

28. Anne Meis Knupfer, "African-American Women's Clubs in Chicago: 1890–1920," Illinois Periodicals Online, Northern Illinois University Library, 2003, http://www.lib.niu.edu/2003/iht1020311.html.

29. Ibid.

30. Ibid.

31. David C. Bartlett and Larry A. McLellan, "The Final Ministry of Amanda Berry Smith: An Orphanage in Harvey, Illinois—1895–1915," Illinois Heritage, Illinois Periodicals Online, Northern Illinois University, 1998.

32. Ibid.

33. Ibid.

34. Ibid.

Chapter 17: Women in Missions

1. Jane Hunter, *The Gospel of Gentility: American Women Missionaries in Turn-of-the-Century China* (New Haven: Yale University Press, 1984), xi.

2. Ibid.

3. Ruth A. Tucker and Walter Liefeld, *Daughters of the Church: Women and Ministry from New Testament Times to the Present* (Grand Rapids: Zondervan, 1987), 291.

4. Hunter, *The Gospel of Gentility*, 11.

5. Ibid., xiii.

6. Tucker and Liefeld, *Daughters of the Church*, 291.

7. Elisabeth Elliot, quoted in Tucker and Liefeld, *Daughters of the Church*, 305.

8. Tucker and Liefeld, *Daughters of the Church*, 305.

9. Ibid., 306.

10. Alma Benedict,"Ladies Department," *The Institute Tie*, Chicago, May 27, 1982.

Chapters 18–20: Virginia Asher

1. "The Work in Chicago," *The Institute Tie* (Nov. 30, 1892) vol. 2, no.2, Archives, Moody Bible Institute, Chicago, 1.

2. Thekla Ellen Joiner, *Sin in the City: Chicago and Revivalism 1880–1920* (University of Missouri, 2007), 94.

3. Erik Larson, *The Devil in the White City* (New York: Vintage Books, 2003), 293.

4. Ibid., 247.

5. Ibid., 254.

6. Ibid., 287.

7. Joiner, *Sin in the City*, 94.

8. Larson, *The Devil in the White City*, 282.

9. Memorial Service Program for Mrs. Virginia Asher, "The Virginia Asher Business Women's Bible Councils of Mrs. Virginia Asher," May 9, 1937, Cincinnati, Ohio, Virginia Asher file, Archives, Wheaton College.

10. Ibid.

11. Ibid.

12. Ibid.

13. Ibid.

14. Ibid.

15. Ibid.

16. Ibid.

17. Ibid.

18. Ibid.

19. Joiner, *Sin in the City*, 93.

20. Helen C. Alexander Dixon, "An Appreciation of Mrs. William Asher," Microfilm Roll 16, Crowell Library Archives, Moody Bible Institute, Chicago.

21. Ibid.

22. "History of the Duluth Bethel," The Duluth Bethel, 2006, http://duluthbethel.org/history.htm.

23. Joiner, *Sin in the City*, 95.

24. Dixon, "An Appreciation of Mrs. William Asher," Microfilm Roll 16.

25. William Asher, Alumnus Report to Moody Bible Institute, Microfilm Roll 16, Crowell Library Archives, Moody Bible Institute, Chicago.

26. Edna Louise Asher Case, "Interview with Edna Louise Asher Case by Robert Shuster," Nov. 2, 1981, Billy Graham Center Archives.

27. "With the Sunday Party," Memorial Service Program for Mrs. Virginia Asher, 8.

28. Ibid.

29. Case, "Interview with Edna Louise Asher Case by Robert Shuster."

30. Winnie Freeman, "Women Stirred by Mrs. Asher," Memorial Service Program for Mrs. Virginia Asher, 9.

31. Ibid., 9.

32. Ibid., 10

33. Carol Forbes, Email, Reneker Museum of Winona History, Feb. 21, 2013.

34. Winnie Freeman, "Women Stirred by Mrs. Asher," Memorial Service Program for Mrs. Virginia Asher, 9.

35. Ibid.

36. Thekla Ellen Caldwell, "Women, Men, and Revival: The Third Awakening in Chicago," PhD dissertation, Univ of Illinois at Chicago, 1991, 50.

37. Ibid.

38. Memorial Service Program for Mrs. Virginia Asher.

39. Case, "Interview with Edna Louise Asher Case by Robert Shuster."

40. Memorial Service Program for Mrs. Virginia Asher.

41. Ibid.

Chapters 21–23: Evangeline Booth

1. Priscilla Pope Levison, "Evangeline Cory Booth," Women Evangelists, 2013.

2. Karen Woods, "Soup, Soap, and Salvation: 125 Years of the Salvation Army in the United States," Acton Commentary (Mar. 9, 2005).

3. P.W. Wilson, *General Evangeline Booth of the Salvation Army* (New York: Charles Scribner's Sons, 1948), 34.

4. Ibid., 41.

5. Ibid.

6. Ibid.

7. Kevin Dixon, "Torquay's Other History: The Salvation Army Riots," Talk Torbay, Jan. 6 2011.

8. "Evangeline Booth," The Salvation Army Website.

9. Evangeline Booth, "The Wounds of Christ," *Songs of the Evangel* (New York: Salvation Army, 1927).

10. Ibid.

11. Wilson, *General Evangeline Booth of the Salvation Army*, 76.

12. Ibid.

13. "About the Salvation Army Leader in the United States Evangeline Booth: History and Biography of the Religious Woman Who Brought the Army to America," Trivia Library.

14. Wilson, *General Evangeline Booth of the Salvation Army*, 110.

15. Ibid.

16. Howard T. Livingston, "Memories of the San Francisco Earthquake and Fire of 1906," The Virtual Museum of the City of San Francisco.

17. Ibid.

18. Herbert A. Wisbey, *Soldiers without Swords* (New York: The MacMillan Company, 1955), 153.

19. Wilson, *General Evangeline Booth of the Salvation Army*, 231.

20. Wisbey, *Soldiers without Swords*, 153.

21. Ibid.

22. Wilson, *General Evangeline Booth of the Salvation Army*, 129.

23. Ibid., 130.

24. Ibid., 141.

25. Levison, "Evangeline Cory Booth," Women Evangelists, 2013.

26. "Evangeline Booth: Orator and Preacher," *The Gazette*, Oct. 16, 1997, Memorial University of Newfoundland's Archival Treasures.

27. Ibid.

28. Kevin Sims, "Salvation Army Marks 100th Anniversary of the Death of Their Founder William Booth," The Salvation Army, Aug. 17, 2012.

29. Richard Collier, *The General Next to God*, Qtd in Kevin Sims, "Salvation Army Marks 100th Anniversary of the Death of Their Founder William Booth."

30. Dan Graves, "Evangeline Cory Booth Spent Her Years for God," Christianity.com, July 2007.

31. "Doughnut! The Official Story" Doughboy Center: The Story of the American Expeditionary Forces, Great War Society, 2000.

32. Wilson, *General Evangeline Booth of the Salvation Army*, 160.

33. Ibid., 148.

34. Ibid. 150

35. Ibid., 155.

36. Ibid., 239

37. Kate Kelly, "Evangeline Booth," Westchester County Historical Society.

38. Evangeline Booth, *Toward a Better World* (New York: Doubleday, 1928), 20.

39. Evangeline Booth, "The World for God," 1934.

Chapter 24: Women and Politics

1. "Reforming Their World: Women in the Progress Era," National Women's History Museum, 2007, http://www.nwhm.org/online-exhibits/progressiveera/wctu.html.

2. Amanda Hedrick, "Progressive Protestantism: the Life of Frances Willard, 1839–1896," The American Religious Experience, West Virginia University, http://are.as.wvu.edu/willard.html.

3. Ruth A. Tucker and Walter Liefeld, *Daughters of the Church: Women and Ministry from New Testament Times to the Present* (Grand Rapids: Zondervan, 1987), 273.

4. Anne Meis Knupfer, *Toward a Tenderer Humanity and a Nobler Womanhood: African American Women's Clubs in Turn-of-the-Century Chicago*, (New York, New York UP, 1996), 9.

Chapters 25–27: Mary McLeod Bethune

1. Jesse Walter Dees Jr., "The College Built on Prayer," Archives, Bethune Cookman Library.

2. Dorothy Walworth, "An Unforgettable Character," Reader's Digest, Feb. 1952:146–52, Mary McLeod Bethune File, Archives, Moody Bible Institute, Chicago.

3. Booker T. Washington, *Up From Slavery: An Autobiography* (New York: Doubleday, 1901). Also available at www.bartleby.com/1004/.

4. Mary McLeod Bethune, "This I Believe," Radio Program, Daily Radio Series Hosted by Edward R. Murrow, Personal Statement, 1954.

5. American Friends Service Committee, Press Release, Philadelphia, PA, Mary McLeod Bethune File, Archives, Moody Bible Institute, Chicago.

6. Walworth, "An Unforgettable Character."

7. Dolores C. Lefall and Janet L. Simms, "Mary McLeod Bethune Annotated Bibliography," *The Journal of Negro Education*.

8. Rackham Holt, *Mary McLeod Bethune: A Biography* (New York: Doubleday, 1964) 41.

9. Walworth, "An Unforgettable Character."

10. Holt, *Mary McLeod Bethune: A Biography*, 43.

11. Walworth, "An Unforgettable Character."

12. Lerone Bennett, Jr. "Mary McLeod Bethune Started College with $1.50 and Faith," Ebony, Dec. 1982, Chronicles of Black Courage Part II: 136-138, Archives, Bethune Cookman, Daytona Beach, FL.

13. Lefall and Simms, "Mary McLeod Bethune Annotated Bibliography," 3.

14. Violet Wood, "Glass Windows," *Pilgrim Youth* (March 1948), Biographical Files, Archives, Moody Bible Institute, 29.

15. Dees Jr., "The College Built on Prayer."

16. Bennett, Jr. "Mary McLeod Bethune Started College with $1.50 and Faith," *Ebony* (Dec. 1982), *Chronicles of Black Courage Part II: 136–38*, Archives, Bethune Cookman, Daytona Beach, FL.

17. Mary McLeod Bethune, "Spiritual Autobiography: 1946," *Mary McLeod Bethune: Building a Better World*, Audrey Thomas McCluskey & Elaine M. Smith, eds., (Bloomington: Indiana UP, 2001), 53.

18. Edward R. Rodriguez, "A Summary of the Life & Works of Our Illustrious Leader," n.d., Archives, Bethune Cookman Library.

19. Walworth, "An Unforgettable Character," 149.

20. Donna Callea, "B-CC Founder's Life Made a Difference," *The News Journal*.

21. Ibid.

22. Ibid.

23. Wood, "Glass Windows," *Pilgrim Youth*, 29.

24. *Mary McLeod Bethune: Building a Better World*, Audrey Thomas McCluskey & Elaine M. Smith, eds. (Bloomington: Indiana UP, 2001), 5.

25. Walworth, "An Unforgettable Character."

26. Rodriguez, "A Summary of the Life & Works of Our Illustrious Leader."

27. Holt, *Mary McLeod Bethune: A Biography*, 191.

28. Ibid., 193.

29. Ibid., 195.

30. Ibid., 181.

31. Walworth, "An Unforgettable Character."

32. Mary McLeod Bethune, "My Last Will and Testament," Archives, Bethune Cookman Library.

33. Mary McLeod Bethune, "My Foundation," *Mary McLeod Bethune: Building a Better World*, Audrey Thomas McCluskey & Elaine M. Smith, eds., (Bloomington: Indiana University Press, 2001), 271.